Best Wishes

Robert K

Raija Ro

OPERATION WAPPEN

Operation Wappen

603 Capitol Ave., Suite 310 Cheyenne, Wyoming USA 82001
-888-980-6523 | admin@urlinkpublishing.com

RLink Print and Media is committed to excellence in the publishing industry.

blished in the United States of America

BN 978-1-64367-531-2 (Paperback)
BN 978-1-64367-530-5 (Digital)

05.19

A WAR THAT NEVER WAS

OPERATION WAPPEN

ROBERT MADDOC

urlink
PRINT & MEDIA

DEDICATION

This history is dedicated to my class mates, instructors and commanders of Basic Class 4-56 and to the men of Fox Battery 2nd Battalion 10th Marines and 3rd Battalion 6th Marines plus all those Finnish men and women with ***sisu*** who fought two brutal wars against Russia (1939-44) and despite overwhelming odds, beat them to stalemate!!

The campaigns described here did not involve hostile action. My wife and illustrator saw real war in Finland during the Continuation War with Russia and was subjected to air attacks. A bomb hit her back yard. She was 15 miles from the front when it ended. Her father, **Anti Olavi Pönkänen** (1913-2000) served in the Finnish Army. His decorations: Winter War (clasp (Kotijoukot), Winter War, Continuation War, and 25 Year War Veterans Association, are pictured.

CONTENTS

FOREWORD

Not long ago my grandniece, Rachael, adopted great granddaughter of Anti Olavi Pönkänen, asked me, "What was "the Cold War all about?" This small book about my experiences is also for her and all other members of our family.

When I was young, even before the mythical James Bond was known, I thought that being a spy or secret agent would be exciting. At various times in life I have met such people. I work with a large corporation that has risk management and security departments. They employ retired ex-FBI and CIA agents. My Father, **Robert K Maddock,** MD FACP (1905-1982), was a physician in the US Public Health Service for 26 years that spanned World War II and the Korean War. He had trained a number of residents in internal medicine. One was Robert Farrier, who became involved with the CIA and served as a physician in a number of embassies. He probably doubled as an intelligence gatherer since he knew Allen Dulles, Director of the CIA, on a first name basis. When I graduated from Stanford University in 1956, I was accepted by several medical schools, but also had an obligation with the NROTC (Naval Reserve Officers Training Corps) to serve 2 years of active duty as a Marine Corps officer.

I put medical training on hold, met my two year active service obligation and served 7 additional years in the ready reserve. My father, with hopes I would go to medical school, purchased a microscope for me. Good ones were made in Germany and difficult to get. He asked Dr. Farrier, if he could get one. He passed the request to Allen Dulles who was about to head for Germany and agreed to get a Zeiss.

He was successful and even used its elegant wooden box as a seat in several military transport planes that carried freight and had no passenger seats. Secret folks don't go commercial.

I began my service at Basic School, Quantico, VA in June 1956 and eventually trained as an artillery officer and served with the 10th Marine Regiment (artillery) at Camp Lejeune, NC. From September to November, 1957 I shipped to the Mediterranean with Fox Battery, 2nd Battalion, 10th Marines (F-2-10) and was attached to the infantry, 3rd Battalion 6th Marine Regiment (3-6) as their "forward observer."

Ostensibly this was to be part of Operation Deep Water, [1] but as I was to learn 50 years later, turned out to be part of a clandestine operation known as Operation Wappen. [2] We knew nothing of Wappen at the time, but had been told that for "administrative purposes" we were still at Camp Lejeune. We continued to pay our monthly rent to the BOQ (bachelor's officers' quarters) and got no overseas or hazardous duty pay, etc.

OPERATIONS DEEP WATER & WAPPEN

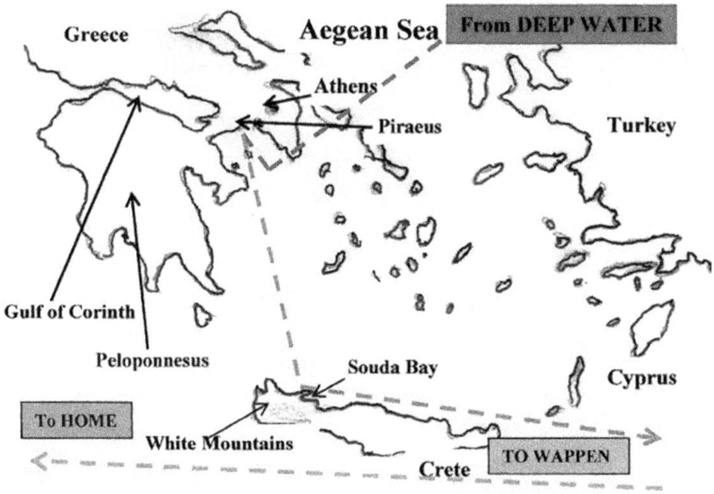

In addition our units were "beefed up" to "full strength" and F-2-10 got two additional 105 mm howitzers, four additional 4.2" mortars and two 8" self-propelled howitzers from Force Troops.

We were told that we were going to Turkey to participate in *Operation Deep Water.* Its purpose was to demonstrate for top NATO officers the first helicopter deployment behind enemy lines of an intact infantry battalion.[3] You may recall that during World War II, paratroopers were used to carry out assignments behind enemy lines. They were used to disrupt enemy forces and eventually join ground troops. The problem was that deploying troops by parachute was perilous and often scattered them to such a degree that they could not fight as an organized unit for several days or more

(D-day / Operation Market Garden). We proved that an entire battalion could be landed intact 20 miles or more behind enemy lines and be ready for immediate deployment as an organized unit.

Following *Deep Water* we were sent to Athens for a 10-day liberty, but on the 8th day (9 October) we were suddenly sent to Souda Bay, Crete for 5 days of conditioning marches in the White Mountains. When we returned to our ships, they were "combat loaded" and we were prepared for a hostile landing on the Syrian Coast scheduled for 17 October 1957.

What made no sense was that we had only "blank" ammunition left over from Operation Deepwater. We had no sooner arrived off the Syrian Coast when without any further notice on the day of the scheduled landing, found ourselves headed for Palermo, Sicily, Barcelona, Gibraltar and home. For years I wondered about the sudden cancelation of our Syrian adventure. Then in 2013 I got curious. I went on line and "Googled" Syria 1957;" up popped "Operation Wappen." [4] It became immediately apparent that this was the real reason we were sent to "the Med" (Mediterranean Sea). Everything I knew about it including the dates fit.

With the help of the Eisenhower Library, I researched White House Meeting Records for September and October of 1957 and found further evidence for my suspicions. Transcripts of these meetings are not available, but the names of those in attendance were. Our real mission was an MI6 (British equivalent of the CIA) and a CIA joint operation to topple the Syrian government. This further led me to investigate the Cold War and the skullduggery going on behind the scenes. My advice to my children about clandestine service is simple. Don't go there!! Being a spy or secret agent can be nothing more than "murder for hire" with an official license to kill from the government. It is a risky business that often leads to premature death, sorrow for your family, personal guilt, and post-traumatic stress. [5] This is a real story.

PATTON'S MURDER & THE "COLD WAR"

On the grounds of Westminster College, Fulton, Missouri stands an unlikely building. It is one of the oldest intact structures in the Western world. It is **St Mary Aldermanbury.** It was built in London about 1181 AD and burned during the London fire of 1666. It was rebuilt by the famous architect, Christopher Wren, but was turned into a ruined shell during the London Blitz of 1940 and remained in that condition until transported block by block in 1966 and rebuilt in Middle America. It is known as the Churchill Memorial Library and commemorates Winston Churchill's "iron curtain" speech of March 5, 1946 in Fulton, Missouri at Westminster College. He began:

"***The United States stands at this time at the pinnacle of world power. It is a solemn moment for the American democracy. For with this primacy in power is also joined an awe-inspiring accountability to the future. As you look around you, you must feel not only the sense of duty done, but also you must feel anxiety lest you fall below the level of achievement. Opportunity is here now, clear and shining, for both our countries. To reject it or ignore it or fritter it away will bring upon us all the long reproaches of the aftertime. It is necessary that constancy of mind, persistency of purpose, and the grand simplicity of decision shall rule and guide the conduct of the English-speaking peoples in peace as they did in war.***"

After complimenting Stalin and the Russians for their war effort he continued, "***It is my duty, however, to place before you certain facts about the present position in Europe. From Stettin in the Baltic to Trieste***

in the Adriatic an iron curtain has descended across the Continent. Behind that line lie all the capitals of the ancient states of Central and Eastern Europe. Warsaw, Berlin, Prague, Vienna, Budapest, Belgrade, Bucharest and Sofia; all these famous cities and the populations around them lie in what I must call the Soviet sphere, and all are subject, in one form or another, not only to Soviet influence but to a very high and in some cases increasing measure of control from Moscow. The safety of the world, ladies and gentlemen, requires a unity in Europe, from which no nation should be permanently outcast." [6]

NATO (North Atlantic Treaty Organization) would follow later. Churchill didn't mention an incident that had occurred 3 months earlier. It is unlikely that he knew anything about it other than from news reports. Churchill had been removed from office 26 July, 1945 and replaced by Clement Attlee of the Socialist Labour Party by the British people in a general election. They were war weary and wanted "change." They got it along with loss of empire, labor unrest, and near bankruptcy that the Thatcher government would try to fix during the 1980s.

The Cold War was a product of its predecessor, the Second World War, also considered a continuation of the First World War. The Second ended and the Cold War began with the wounding and then death of one of the most celebrated heroes of any war, **General George Smith Patton Jr.** (1885-1945)

Clandestine operations during war have been present since the beginning of the world's second oldest profession – soldiering. All armies employ assassins – "James Bond 007" types. These are not "snipers" in uniform who along with artillery forward observers perform some of the riskiest jobs on the battlefield. They are plain clothes guys or gals, who if caught are often tortured first then summarily executed. The Bible even describes such a person. Ehud who was "*left-handed*" (meaning an assassin) managed to kill Eglon, the King of Moab (Jordan). He delivered Israel from its grasp (Judges 3:15-30). World War II was no different. The U.S. Army had its CIC (Counterintelligence Corps) and OSS (Office of Strategic Services); the Russians had their NKVD (*Narodny Komissarat Vnutrennikh Del*).

The only difference between World War II and ancient times was the level of sophistication. Traffic accidents and hospitals were now convenient venues for assassinations. [7] Patton must have known that someone was out to kill him. On April 20, 1945 while returning to his headquarters in his light aircraft, an unarmed single engine, L-5 Sentinel, a Spitfire with Polish markings made 3 strafing runs against his aircraft and missed. Because of the skill of Patton's pilot the Spitfire came in too close to the ground and crashed on the third run. No British or Polish Spitfires were operating in the region, but the Russians owned many. [8] Two weeks later another possible attempt to kill him occurred when a peasant ox-cart narrowly missed running into his jeep. It had a protruding farm tool tipped with a sharpened blade that narrowly missed the General. [9, 10]

According to recent evidence, Patton was involved in a deliberately planned traffic accident on 9 December 1945 in which he was severely wounded with an alleged paralyzing pistol shot to the neck delivered by OSS officer, **Douglas DeWitt Bazata** (1911-1999). The back seat of the car where Patton sat was full of blood, atypical for an accident with a simple neck fracture. It had been ordered and paid for by OSS Chief, **William J. "Wild Bill" Donovan** (1883-1959).

Donovan was not trusted by President Truman, General MacArthur, and many other high officials. Within months his OSS was disbanded and although a genuine war hero (CMH, DSC, Silver Star, 3 purple hearts), he never again found himself in public service. He had planned the postwar CIA (Central Intelligence Agency) and wanted to lead it, but his deputy, Allen Dulles, would have that honor.

Patton died in a Heidelberg hospital, while paralyzed and unguarded possibly due to a cyanide injection or spray gun [11] on 21 December 1945 allegedly administered by a Soviet NKVD operative under orders from General Alexander M. Dāvidov. There were more witnesses to the crime. Many ended up dead within a few years including Dāvidov. They "knew too much."

Stephen J. Skubik (1919/5-1996) US Army CIC (Counterintelligence Corps) attached to 3rd Army, published a book in 1993, *The Murder of General Patton.* [It is available only on line.[12]]

Skubik's friend and fellow spy from the Ukrainian Army, **Stepan Andrivovych Bandera** (1909 – 1959), also a later victim of assassination, had found Patton on an NKVD "hit list." [13] Finally there was Bert C Roosen, a German laborer working in Eisenhower's rail car who eventually fled to Canada, and Robert L. Thompson (died 1994), the driver of the truck that hit Patton's car.

There is plenty of circumstantial evidence from multiple sources to corroborate these seemingly outrageous claims, but physical evidence is lacking and most of the reports pertaining to the accident have mysteriously disappeared. Even the "Patton car" at Fort Knox was a fake – 1939 Cadillac instead of 1938, VIN numbers filed off, and no evidence of the blood reported at the time. [14] The real car has disappeared. There was no autopsy. A court conviction would be difficult. [15]

Why Patton? He also "knew too much." 3rd Army had the best intelligence service of all the armies in the war and Patton attended their daily briefings. This was one of the secrets of his success. He had little respect for the Russians. He called them "Barbarians" and "Mongols." He knew Stalin's plans to take Eastern European countries as Soviet satellites. President Roosevelt, then sick and dying, sold out to the Soviets and prevented the US and British armies from taking Berlin. Ike who had initially told Generals Patton and Hodges to take Czechoslovakia suddenly cancelled it on orders "from above."

Patton also knew about numerous military blunders, peccadillos, and political aspirations of top US and British commanders. Eisenhower was "political" and "in bed" with the British. He had trained troops, but never served in a direct combat billet. Bradley was too cautious and gullible. Montgomery was so cautious he was almost paralytic, but was favored by Ike because he was British. Patton knew about Ike and Kay Summersby, a British secret agent sent to have an affair and influence him. Ike had missed an opportunity to end the war at the Falaise pocket (12-21 August 1944) by stopping Patton from doing it while giving the job to Montgomery. The over-cautious Montgomery failed to close it allowing 50-100,000 Germans to escape. Patton said:

"A good plan violently executed now is better than a perfect plan executed next week."

"Monty's" caution also failed at Market Garden. Patton warned Bradley about *"Herbstnebel" the* German code name for the impending "Battle of the Bulge" weeks before it happened, but Bradley laughed it off. Like Longstreet during our Civil War (See Henry Thomas Harrison.[16]), Patton had agents on the ground behind enemy lines. These debacles had cost unnecessary Allied lives and prolonged the war. Patton also knew that Washington, London and Moscow were crawling with spies, agents and double agents. The NKVD (Russian secret service) had agents deeply imbedded at the highest levels of government in Washington such as Lt

Col. Duncan Chaplin Lee (1913-1988), Harry Hopkins (1890-1946), and Harry Dexter White (1892-1948) of International Monetary Fund and World Bank fame. Even MI6 was infiltrated. [17] There were many others. [18] [19]

Patton wasn't afraid to tell all under proper circumstances and was planning to resign his commission and speak out. He was fatally injured the day before his scheduled departure for home. He was independently wealthy and never collected his military pay from the time he was a 1st Lt. He could not be bought and he knew way too much, and, as noted, had been targeted for assassination twice before.

I have reviewed what is known of the hospital records and agree that a pulmonary embolism may have killed General Patton. He had had a horse accident in 1937 that broke his right leg that caused phlebitis. This could have created a potential nidus from which a clot might develop. His hospital course and x-ray examinations, still available, were all compatible with a pulmonary embolus, but what might have caused it is the mystery. Only an exhumation will be able to prove the theories surrounding his likely murder.

The evidence has been recently examined and amply explained in two excellent books: ***Target Patton: the Plot to Assassinate General George S. Patton*** by Robert K Wilcox. Regnery Publishing, Inc. Washington DC. 2008 and ***Killing Patton: The Strange Death of World War II's Most Audacious General*** by Bill O'Reilly and Martin Dugard, Henry Holt & Co., New York 2014. *Target Patton* gives intimate detail about those involved in the conspiracy and their activities in the alleged assassination. *Killing Patton* provides more World War II background and associated detail, but is less involved with the assassins.

A third excellent source for those who want more information about the General is the 2 volume set, ***The Patton Papers*** by Martin Blumenson, Houghton Mifflin Co. Boston. 1974. These give Patton's history in his own words from Diaries and letters. It was ironic that Patton's statement, "***There's only one proper way for a professional soldier to die: the last bullet of the last battle of the last war***", may have come true. [20] The shot that wounded him made him the last casualty of World War II and his alleged death by an NKVD [21] assassin was the first casualty of the Cold War.

The Cold War, frequently "hot", included Soviet support of the Chinese Revolution under Mao Zedong ending in a Communist takeover in 1949, the Korean War (1950-3), the Vietnam revolution under Ho Chi Minh against the French (1946-54), the US–Vietnam War (1955-75), Bay of Pigs (Apr. 1961), Cuban Missile Crisis (Oct 1962), Grenada (Oct 1983), Russo-Afghan War (1979-89), and the removal of the Berlin Wall (1989). Finally there was the Gulf War (2 Aug 1990 – 28 Feb 1991) that proved the fallacy of Soviet military prowess and led to its temporary retreat. There were also other near misses in terms of overt total war that included incidents such as these.

The events of 1956-7 in the Middle East encouraged by Soviet money and diplomacy re-ignited an ancient war that had been quiescent since the Crimean War ended in 1856. It began an economic decline and the rise of the "Young Turks" that led to the fall of the Ottoman Empire in 1923. It was reignited in 1956, 100 years after its pause following the Crimean War (1856), when Egypt using Soviet money armed and equipped Jordanian Fedayeen Terrorists to raid Israel. 5 sporadic acts of terrorism occurred between 1956 and 1970. [22] At that time oil money swelled the coffers of several Islamic states and acts of terror became far more frequent. [23]

Egypt's seizure of the Suez Canal encouraged by the Soviets in 1956 led to the Arab-Israeli War, Britain, France and Israel against Egypt – more on this later. A bi-partite agreement between Egypt and Syria – the pending United Arab Republic–combining their armies under Egyptian control with Soviet support caused anxiety in both London and Washington. France had lost Vietnam to a Communist takeover two years earlier and before that, China had "gone Red" with Soviet help. In the summer of 1956 with the seizure of the Suez Canal, it seemed possible that the Middle East would also "go Red." Efforts to stabilize the Middle East were plagued with uncertainty and confusion, but it was a game "for keeps." At the same time in Saudi Arabia a proud father and billionaire businessman, Mohammed bin Awad bin Laden, had a 7 month-old baby boy. 44 ½ years later he would carry the 1300 Years' War to the heart of New York City on the anniversary of the height of the Ottoman Empire, 11 September 1683 at the gates of Vienna. **Osama bin Laden** (1957 – 2011) was one of the first and certainly the most notorious of modern knights. Like those of old he was supported by princes and kings with common religious goals to attack foreign interests. It is again a war between Middle Eastern Islam and the West, a 1300 Years' War." [24]

THE GODS

Beliefs have always influenced man. To deny this is to deny the history of mankind from its beginnings. Man has worshiped himself, nature, idols (Deut 4:28), and God. This includes sun, moon and stars (Deut: 4:16-19). God was often ethereal or in human form. To understand history and current events we must understand how people think. Nowadays this means a working knowledge of our major ideologies– Judeo-Christianity, Islam, and Communist-socialism. These are represented by the *Bible*, *Korân*, and *the Manifesto of the Communist Party* by Marx and Engels. Diplomats who don't know these sources from the standpoint of a believer will be incompetent. Marx studied Rousseau and rejected his own Judeo-Christian background and championed an ideology of revolution and collectivism. As it developed, this required "strong-man" leadership. By the end of the 20th Century these three belief systems influenced all the world's governments, their ideology and laws. Belief systems have been important since ancient times. Tyrants after accumulating great wealth have used their philosophers and religious leaders to whip up their people to war.

Tyranny comes in many forms political and religious. Our Founders feared and mistrusted government and fashioned one that would interfere as little as possible with its citizens. They believed that God created man with a mind that can change and think abstractly with language. They relied on "Divine Providence" for protection.

In its second paragraph, our *Declaration of Independence* makes this statement, "*We hold these truths to be self-evident, that all men are created equal, that they are endowed by their Creator with certain unalienable Rights, that among these are Life, Liberty and the pursuit of Happiness.*" It ends with this statement: "*And for the support of this Declaration, with a firm reliance on the protection of Divine Providence, we mutually pledge to each other our Lives, our Fortunes, and our sacred Honor.*"

There is no other creature on the face of the earth with this potential. Some animals can be domesticated, trained, and even act on prior experience. Some like insects are "hard-wired," but mankind can reprogram himself from within his own mind. In religious terms, he can "repent" or change his mind provided he does not destroy it with various substances or trauma. This is part of the "truth" that "make you free" (John 8:32, 36). It is one of the basic doctrines of Christianity, but not of socialism or Islam.

Man is not a plaything of the Gods directed by determinism (a secular term) or predestination (a religious term). He has choice and stewardship to which he will be held accountable. (Matt 25:14-30) This is what makes him as the Gods, and he can't do it in Utopia / Eden (Gen 3:22-23). These ancient Judeo-Christian concepts are true and are behind European Western Civilization. Attack or destroy Christianity and you commit Western Civilization's suicide.

In the determinist world, man becomes the tool of priests and tyrants that guide him using armies, laws, police, selective taxation, penalties and propaganda. See 1 Samuel 8. Under these conditions progress and happiness are stifled. When the Semitic Code of Hammurabi–"an eye for an eye" or Lex Talionis, law of revenge (just to make it "fair") is added, bloodshed occurs. Islam is heavily invested in both predestination ("God wills it.") and Lex Talionis ("killings").[25] These beliefs also have been part of sectarian Judeo-Christianity. This denies man's nature, stewardship and personal responsibility. Marxist socialism has been tried in numerous places and conditions. It always fails. Where it has been tried on a large scale, it has led to poverty, chaos, and evil; it is economically unsustainable.

BACKGROUND

The collapse of the Western Roman Empire in the 5th and 6th Centuries was followed by the Rise of Islam in the 7th Century. Islam's control of the Silk Road, Persian Gulf, and Red Sea by 640 AD began an isolation of Europe from the Far East. This nurtured the Dark Age and lasted 900 years through medieval times. It was not broken until the Mongol Invasions of the late 13th Century and Timurids invasion of the early 15th Century. Only Marco Polo (1254-1354), his father and uncle made it to China via the Silk Road during the chaos of the Mongol period and Niccolò de' Conti (1395-1469) traded in the Indian Ocean shortly following the chaos of the Timurids. About the time of de' Conte information in the form of maps and star charts [26] made their way into the hands of the Pope and Templar Grand Master, Infante Dom Henrique de Avis, Duke of Viseu or Henry the Navigator (1394-1460). There followed the Great Age of Exploration and the Renaissance of the 15th and 16th Centuries in Europe. The printing press (1450) and the Reformation (1522-1546), marked the end of the Medieval Period and Roman Catholic domination in the West.

At the time of Jamestown and the beginning of the British Empire (1607) war and thought were changing. 75 years earlier the death of **Franz von Sickingen** (1481-1523) ended the power of knights. Gunpowder, artillery, and large armies were too expensive for them; only kings could afford war and conduct diplomacy. The 30 Years' War (1618-48) destroyed the German principalities, but established Protestantism and modern gunpowder war.

Franz von Sickingen

The Crimean War (1853-6) sent the Ottoman Empire into major decline. It finally ended in 1923. This spelled the temporary end of the Islamic Caliphate and wars with the West. One of the goals of the Paris Peace Conference of 1919 besides "punishing the Hun" was "dismantling the Turk." This meant dividing up the Ottoman Empire and turning various "mandates" over to allied "trustees." France got Algeria, Lebanon & Syria. Italy got Libya, England got Palestine and Egypt and the Saudi's got to keep their own land because of oil contracts with the British. The German Empire was similarly divvied up. The US got German – now American – Samoa. Presently, the caliphate is undergoing a revival of both Sunni (Muslim Brotherhood) and Shia (Iran) branches. Both include powerful elements that are determined to exterminate each other along with Christians and Jews. They want to drive Jews from the Holy Land, and spread fundamentalist Islam to the world including Europe and the Americas.

In 1945 war changed again with the beginning of the atomic age. With the end of World War II, less expensive weapons of mass destruction permitted "knights" with outside support, to re-enter the battlefield. These took the form of "terrorists." There were two super powers. The USA and USSR operated from different philosophical and religious perspectives.

History has shown us that warfare changes depending on the availability of technology and skill of army commanders. In the ancient world it was patterned after the formations developed by Alexander the Great and others with line, column, phalanx and cavalry. Orders were simple and not changed. High ground with wind at your back was most desirable. With the advent of gunpowder, siege guns and hand held muskets, heavy armor and fortresses became obsolete. Field artillery was in. Improved logistics increased the numbers on the battlefield. With railroads, telegraphs, modern medical services, barbed wire and machine guns, defensive trench warfare began. The battlefield could include a country's entire frontier and about 10 miles on either side. Most of the damage of World War I was confined to a 60 mile strip inside the northern French border. With aircraft, tanks, trucks, and radios, plans could be more complex and movement more fluid. With the helicopter, demonstrated in 1957 at Operation Deep Water, battle fields increased in depth (100 – 200 miles) and movement became more fluid. In the modern era, sophisticated communication, unmanned military vehicles on the ground and in the air, relatively inexpensive weapons of mass destruction [improvised explosive devices – IEDs, gas, bacterial warfare, cyber-attacks, "dirty bombs"] and more fluid national borders have changed the battlefield again. It is now **your entire country**. Targets are usually "soft," undefended and civilian. The knights that went out of style in 1522 are back in the form of tribal chiefs, mercenaries, and cartels often in cahoots with national governments, princes and kings. Just as in days of yore, they commit atrocities, assassinations, kidnappings, and hold people hostage for ransom. In general they run amok terrorizing the neighborhood.

Small "hit squads," like the knights and their squires, work for the highest bidder. Sometimes they have little loyalty to any particular king, prince, dictator, or national boundary. At other times they have loyalty to some form of ideology (Marx or Islam). We are even seeing the return of mercenaries in the form of "private contractors." Economic chaos in the West may see well trained soldiers switching sides bought by private entities and countries that can afford them. This happened at the end of the Roman Empire. To be successful in this era of "irregular" or 4th generation warfare will require "hard money" and generals who can find unique ways to carry it out.

Cooperative socialist-like Christian religious groups began the monastic system. In the 19th Century socialist ideology spread in the United States and Europe–Robert Owen's Harmony in Great Britain and New Harmony in the United States. Both failed. George Rapp's Lutheran Harmony near Pittsburgh and the Shakers were other examples. Marxist socialism began its first trial in Bismarck's Germany in the 1880s. It collapsed with World War I and the hyperinflation following it, but was replaced by the National Socialist Worker's Party – Nazism – in the mid1930s. This was a copy of a similar system developed in Italy by Mussolini in the 1920s and similar to Francisco Franco's Spanish brand 1939-75. Germany, Italy and Spain utilized a form of crony-capitalism under state tyrannical control. In the U.S. Medicare and forms of state sponsored environmentalism, Federal Reserve banking and commerce control is a "lite" form of the same. The USSR tried an international brand of purer Marxism under Lenin in 1917 with direct state control of all the major means of production. It eventually rejected Christian and Islamic religious beliefs. Italy and Spain held to Roman Catholicism while Germany was hostile to Judaism and unfriendly to Christianity. Both Germany and the USSR was expansionist.

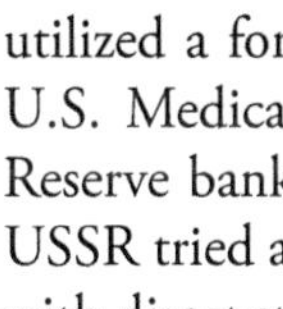

Russia had been expansionist since **Ivan the Terrible (1547-1584)**. The USSR under Lenin and Stalin wanted world-wide communism. Hitler also wanted more territory but he had a more limited brand of socialism or Nazism. Tyrannies often include two ancient beliefs:

1. Lex talionis (the law of retaliation) from the Code of Hammurabi–"an eye for an eye," a form of "fairness;" one bad deed deserves another.

2. Determinism or predestination – a denial of "free-will."

Predestination espoused by Luther and Calvin was blended with a modified socialism sometimes known in Europe as Christian-Democrat, a blend of Marxism and scripture. Marx's erroneous philosophy of finite resources and zero-sum economics fooled the gullible and spread misery.

The United States, with many free, non-sectarian, Christian congregations, was founded on Protestant Christian beliefs. These included Christ as a peace maker and Savior, free choice, markets, individual stewardship, and permission to lend and collect interest (Matt 25:14-30), plus the importance of families with solid marriages (Matt 19:6; Mark 10:9). It favored a democratic republic with separation of powers and a union of separate states similarly organized. States held most of the power. The Federal government conducted foreign affairs, created "hard" money, built post-roads, and defended the whole. The framers of the US Constitution held to Christian beliefs espoused in the *Declaration of Independence* – "endowed by their Creator with certain unalienable rights." Christianity also rejected the law of retaliation (Mat: 5:38-41) and promoted free will and stewardship, but not "fairness." [See parables of the sower, laborers in the vineyard, the ten virgins, "talents," and prodigal son (Mat: 13:3-9; 20:1-16; 25:1-13; 25:14-30; Luke 15:11-32) none of this was "fair."] This is also in line with the biological 80-20 rule or Pareto principle. [27] There will always be "the poor" (Mat 26:11; Mark 14:7; John 12:8). What matters is how we as individuals respond to them. The founders mistrusted any government of man and knew it had to be tightly controlled. Christian principles became the basis of the representative republican form of government in the United States, but sectarian Christianity and any other form of church sponsorship was outlawed. No particular brand of Christianity or other religious beliefs would be permitted to directly control national or state governments. Warfare (national & corporate) of the mid to late 19th Century and all of the 20th Century increased Federal Government's power.

At the time of its colonization, 80-95% of the Native Americans had died of disease. [28] During famines and times of reduced immunity millions of Europeans had died of the Black Death (1346-1353), but the percentages were about half that of the Native Americans. [29] During early colonial times plague killed many more in England (1563, 1593, 1603, 1625, 1636, 1665), Italy (1630) and Germany (1709-30). However, Europeans held the military advantage of an advanced civilization with literacy, iron-age metallurgy, advanced logistical methods, and labor saving domestic animals. Both groups included the evils of slavery common then and now.

Between 1607 and 1661 the colonists rejected chattel slavery and used indentured servitude as a way of paying debt. Then the king's ministers brought chattel slavery (cheap labor) as an institution to the colonies and a way to generate more wealth. The *Declaration of Independence* penned by Jefferson included reference to this. It was removed by representatives from the South. [30] Slavery is a terrible economic system. It discourages the slaves and makes slobs of the overseers or as Alexis de Tocqueville observed, "***Slavery ... dishonors labor; it introduces idleness into society, and with idleness, ignorance and pride, luxury and distress. It enervates the powers of the mind and benumbs the activity of man.***" [31]

In its early history, the United States was expansionist. It displaced or assimilated what was left of the primitive people. It bought Louisiana from the French and Florida from the Spanish. It transplanted Indian tribes from south to west.

Then it fought a war against Mexico, conquered all of it, but gave half of it back and then paid for conquered lands and made all who lived there free citizens. The largest town in Alta California in August 1846 was Los Angeles with a total population of 3500; there were about 9000 Californios and 3000 US citizens (Mormons) in Alta California about the time gold was discovered in 1847. [32] The number of Native Americans was unknown. Unlike any other nation from 1861-65 it had fought a terrible war to free slaves, but then it killed the buffalo and drove Indians into collectivist poverty ridden "reservations." By 1960 it decried empire building and gave freedom to all its extra continental territories that asked for it, notably the Philippines (July 4, 1946). Other territories could remain as such, become states, or go their own way. American Samoa, Puerto Rico, Virgin Islands, Northern Marianas, and Guam chose territorial or quasi territorial status. Hawaii and Alaska became states in 1959.

Following its revolution in 1917, Russia (USSR) rejected Orthodox Christianity and adopted Marxism. There was no savior or god. They believed that "capitalism" a made up word to mean modern banking or using money to make money and "free markets" were evil. They weren't "fair." They favored a more mercantilist model under state control allegedly for the benefit of all. It turned out to benefit "the Party." [Read ***Animal Farm*** by George Orwell.] They rejected the family as a "capitalist tool" to exploit women and children. They promoted "free love." Children belonged to the state, not family, and needed "social studies," not history, indoctrination in public institutions, and declared that, "*The history of all hitherto existing society is the history of class struggles.*" [33] They advocated "women in common" and the abolition of family, national boundaries, morality, religion, and eternal truths. [34]

Russia as the USSR held to their expansionism and justified it as "International Communism." They revised their history to make it based on "class struggle." At the Hoover Library, the ***Great Soviet Encyclopedia*** 1926 to 1990 got regular changes so frequently that it was kept in loose-leaf binders. Old pages removed were to be destroyed before new ones were inserted. When I studied there, the Hoover Library kept the old pages and filed them. In 2002 it came back as the *Bolshaya Rossiyskaya Entsiklopediya* or Great Russian Encyclopedia.

They favored any form of chaos or revolt that permitted the advance of communism or as Rahm Emanuel put it, "**You *Never want a serious crisis go to waste.***" [35] This adds tactics to Part IV of the Manifesto of the Communist Party that declares: "***The Communists everywhere support every revolutionary movement against the existing social and political order of things.***" [36] Dictators and oligarchies were the preferred governments. By the time of their revolution the USSR (Great Russia) held the Ukraine (Little Russia), much of the old Polish-Lithuanian Commonwealth including Belarus and the Baltic States. During the 1917 Revolution they lost Finland, the Karelian Isthmus and the Baltic States (formerly under Swedish control). Russian conquest of Siberia began in the 16th Century and progressed through the 17th. It pushed into North America in the 18th century and included Alaska, West Coast Canada and extended as far south as the Russian River in northern California. Claims in North America were vacated when the U.S. purchased Alaska 1867.

Russia also developed its spheres of influence and conquests further south into Central and Eastern Asia in the 19th Century (Kazakhstan, Uzbekistan, Turkmenistan, Kyrgyzstan and Tajikistan). All except Kazakhstan became important when cotton exports from the Southern US dried up during the Civil War (1861-65). In the mid and late 19th Century Russia clashed with British influence in India, Tibet, northern China, Persia, and south of the Caucasus. [37] [38] Massive cotton and other agricultural collectives of the 1960s shrank the Aral Sea to insignificance.

The sand box of the Arabian Peninsula was not attractive to anyone other than archeologists until oil was discovered early in the 20th Century by British and U.S. interests. However the vestiges of the Islamic Ottoman Empire remained in secularist Turkey and among small groups of revolutionaries in Egypt, Arab states and exiles in France. Islam believed in a determinist god responsible for good and evil, the law of retaliation, expansion of its religion, and polygamist families. It rejected usury. It believed that priest craft combined with statecraft and the military (a Caliphate) was the way governments should operate. It had been that way at the time of Muhammad. From its founding in 620 AD until the Crimean War (1853-6) it had waged an almost continuous war of expansion against its neighbors. It expanded into the Middle East, North Africa, the Iberian Peninsula, Central Europe, Central Asia, the Indian sub-continent, and Southeast Asia. It had attempted to suppress Christianity wherever it was. In the Far East it had an uneasy truce with China based on trade, but there was periodic warfare in western China and as far south and east as Canton.

When the two socialist giants of Europe, Germany and Soviet Russia came to blows in World War II, Russia and its mostly Christian Western allies won. In the last year of the war (1944-5) the USSR used its army to gobble up the rest of Central and Eastern Europe, plus Manchuria and half of Korea. By then, much of Europe had combined Marxism with Christian beliefs to form Christian-Democrat political parties. There church bells ring, but few participate.

Most of the Post War Presidents with the exception of Eisenhower, Reagan and GHW Bush, and Trump tended to politicize wars. They either did not know or believe Sun Tzu (544-496 Bc) who warned,

"There has never been a protracted war from which a country has benefited." [39] ***or that able generals should not be constrained by civil government."*** [40]

In the US, Presidents are Commanders in Chief of the Armed Forces and get to nominate "General Officers" and Secretaries of War or Defense. If they fail to pick "fighting generals," and knowledgeable Secretaries, and the Congress fails to use its "advice and consent" powers, or if they attempt to play a major role in military decision making there can be problems. Grenada (1983) under Reagan and Casper Weinberger and the Gulf War under President GHW Bush I and Dick Cheney, were quick and decisive as far as they went. In both General "Storm'n" Norman Schwarzkopf (1934-2012) was field commander. Korea, Vietnam, Iraq and Afghanistan were fought in a "politically correct" manner with impossible "rules of engagement." Korea, Iraq and Afghanistan linger on in uncertainty. Winning allows the victors to dictate the terms. Armistice is a stalemate; no one wins. All this may be changing under President Trump, who seems to understand these principles better than his predecessors.

President GH Bush responded to a direct attack against the US by Al-Qaeda and its most notorious knight, Osama bin Laden. However, ending the war successfully was not permitted by foolish "rules of engagement" and the politics of the time. Most wars become evil and cruel; it's their nature.

THE MARINE CORPS

In his book, *No Bended Knee: the Battle for Guadalcanal*,[41] **General Merrill B Twining**, USMC (1902-1996) writes a chapter, "A Way You'll Never Be." The title came from a Hemingway short story on "siege mentality" or "battle fatigue" during the Spanish Civil War. In the course of action on Guadalcanal between August and December 1942 many became sick.

By November, the rains came. Clothing and equipment were moldy. Supplies were short. Food was foul and water stank. Thousands of unburied Japanese lay rotting in the wet lands surrounding the Marine's perimeter. The stench was horrible. Almost all had malaria and were under treatment with Atabrine which turned skin a ghastly yellow. This masked the jaundice from hepatitis also present in the camp. Despite casualties the enemy was not subdued and was an ever present threat. Seasoned veteran officers, many to become famous in their own right, were seeing "purple shadows" in the night. These were imagined enemy for which heavy concentrations of artillery fire or tank support was requested.

"Battle fatigue" or "traumatic stress syndrome" had caught up to many of all ranks, including Commanding General, **Alexander Vandegrift** (1887-1973 – CMH, Navy Cross, DSM). This is one of the true, but usually ignored stories of the Marine Corps. Despite this, the 1st Marine Division's alert field grade officers including Lt. Col. Merrill B. Twining, the Division's chief of operations, held together, did not waver or obey what were temporarily imprudent orders.

Despite complaints from their front line commanders they usually ignored the "purple shadows," got out of their bunkers, examined the situation and prevailed. They also protected General Vandergrift until he recovered. The Chapter "A Way You'll Never Be" suggests situations that exist, but are not supposed to exist according to common lore. Operation Wappen described here fits this description.

Lt. General Merrill B. Twining, Commandant of Marine Corps Schools, Quantico was my commanding officer at Basic School (Class 4-56). His first assignment after his Basic School in 1923 was with the 10th Marine Regiment (artillery). He was also the brother of General Nathan F Twining, USAF (1897-1982), who would become Chairman of the Joint Chiefs of Staff and would figure prominently in this story.

General Vandergrift later became Commandant of the Marine Corps in 1947. At that time the Army and the Truman administration were determined to "unify" the Marine Corps into insignificance. President Truman had served as an artillery battery commander (Captain) during World War I and had risen to Colonel in the Reserves.

General Vandergrift and members of the "Chowder Society" Brig Gen. Gerald Thomas, Col. Merrill B. Twining, Lt. Col. Victor Krulak, Brig. Gen. Merritt Edson, and 13 others put their careers and reputations on the line in a political struggle defending the Corps. They finally prevailed. [42] Belleau Wood, Guadalcanal, the flag raising on Mount Suribachi, Iwo Jima and the Battle of Chosin Reservoir, Korea (Nov-Dec 1950) [43] are iconic battles demonstrating the fighting spirit of the Corps that persists to this day. It was this reputation – *Semper Fidelis* – that saved the Marine Corps in the halls of Congress. I want my children to know that some of my most cherished memories have to do with service in the Marine Corps. It is here, as is found in most serious military organizations and not commonly in "civilian life," that John 15:13 is often best exemplified,

"Greater love hath no man than this, that a man lay down his life for his friends."

It is no accident that Christ and later Paul found Roman Centurions humble, believing, and helpful (Matt 8 & 27; Mar 15; Luke 7 & 23; Acts 10, 22, 24, 27 & 28). As for most who have served in this illustrious Corps, it is a mark of accomplishment that stays with those who have experienced it for the rest of their lives and gives rise to the saying, "***Once a Marine; always a Marine***."

2nd Lt Earl S Maeser 4-56

Marines have existed for as long as battles at sea have been. They were numerous when ships were oar powered. Their numbers dwindled during the time of sail. Marines were soldiers at sea who fought from the "tops" with rifles or muskets picking off officers and men on the decks of opposing ships. Admiral Lord Horatio Nelson (1758-1805) was fatally wounded by a French Marine's musket shot from the mizzentop of the *Redoutable* during the Battle of Trafalgar. Marines were used as naval landing forces in efforts to take ports and forts. This was how they were known from the time of the Revolutionary War until now. They participated in taking Tripoli during our first undeclared war with the Barbary Pirates in the early 19th Century. They gained the name of Devil Dogs in World War I at Belleau Wood, near Chateau-Thierry, France in June 1918.

One of the units engaged in this fight was 3-6 (3rd Battalion, 6th Marines) to which I was attached during Operations Deep Water and Wappen. Marines became masters of amphibious warfare in the Pacific during WWII and much of what they learned was used during landings in North Africa, Sicily, Italy and Normandy. In my opinion, had LVTs (landing vehicle tracked), been used at Omaha Beach and in the flooded lowlands, the casualties might have been considerably less and the advance much quicker. 3rd Battalion 6th Marines won its Presidential Unit Citation at Tarawa. [44] Without LVTs, that battle would have been in doubt.

In 1952 when I first arrived at Stanford at age 18, the Korean War was in progress. My father told me that if I wanted to stay in school, I had best sign up with a reserve officers' unit as soon as possible. So I signed with the NROTC.

Summer 1953 Norfolk VA
Lawrence, Jensen, Goodell, Griffin, Maddock

I was a midshipman for 2 years, and then concerns over sea-sickness and my respect for its history prompted me to select the Marine Corps Option.

Nuclear war begun in 1945 was maturing. Many in both the US and USSR believed that money could be saved by reducing the size of armies and using the "nuclear option" where there was more "bang for the buck." By 1953 both sides had "tactical" nuclear shells that could be fired from 8" (203 mm) artillery. The problem was that big bangs have big side effects.

Just before graduation on 10 May 1956 I received orders to report not later than 2400 18 June 1956 to the Commandant of Marine Corps Schools, Quantico, Virginia for a physical exam. At graduation on 1 June 1956 I had received my commission as a 2nd Lt.

With physical passed and shots received, we reported to the supply shed for boots and "782 gear" (issued on DD Form # 782). I received my M-1 and was assigned to India Company 1st platoon.

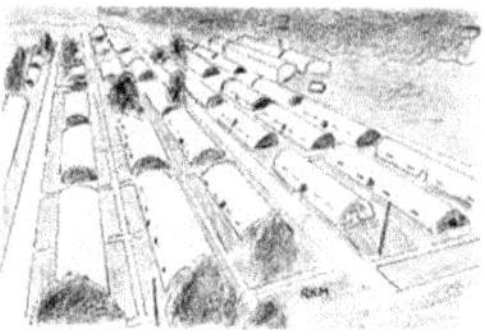

Basic Class 4-56 was at **Camp Upshur,** a collection of Quonset Huts and other steel frame buildings.

Our next task was to obtain uniforms. We were bussed into Washington, DC to Wilmer's where we were fitted out for our greens and khakis. These would cost us about $800 without the optional dress blues – about $400 more. With our pay at about $190 per month, it would take most of our 32 weeks scheduled training to pay for them. However there was little else on which to spend money.

An early interest in photography allowed me to become one of three photographers at Basic School for our class year-book. I carried a camera and was permitted to photograph almost anything. I maintain a collection of 230 pictures taken during that period. Several appear in this work.

Within 3 months of our arrival at Basic School war broke out in the Middle East and rumors circulated that our training might change to war-time standards – 4 months. However, Ike assured the nation there would be "***no US involvement***;" he was as good as his word. There were 316 of us 2nd lieutenants in Basic Class 4-56. All were college graduates and 5 had law degrees. Our class was organized into 2 companies (H & I). There were 170 in H Company divided into 4 platoons of about 43 each; all the lawyers were in H Company.

My last name was in the middle of the alphabet; thus I found myself in

I Company commanded by **Major David A Clement** (1924-2007). He had received a silver star in Korea and was distinguished Pistol shooter." He was a fine descent man. There were 146 in I Company organized into three platoons of about 49 each. I was in the first platoon under **Captain G.V. Ruos Jr.**; he was tough, fair, and concerned about our wellbeing. Both exemplified the Marine Corps moto – "*Semper Fidelis,*" Always *Faithful.* Our quarters at Upshur were Quonset huts. In our **squad bay** each had a locker box and stand up locker into which everything we owned or were issued was supposed to fit neatly. Each platoon occupied a single Quonset hut. We slept two deep in iron double decker beds.

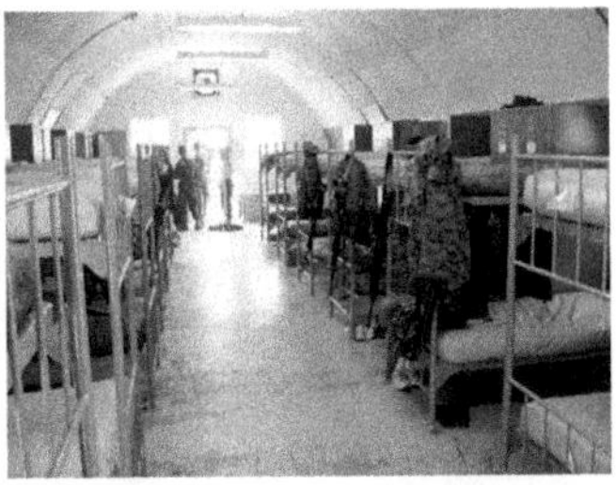

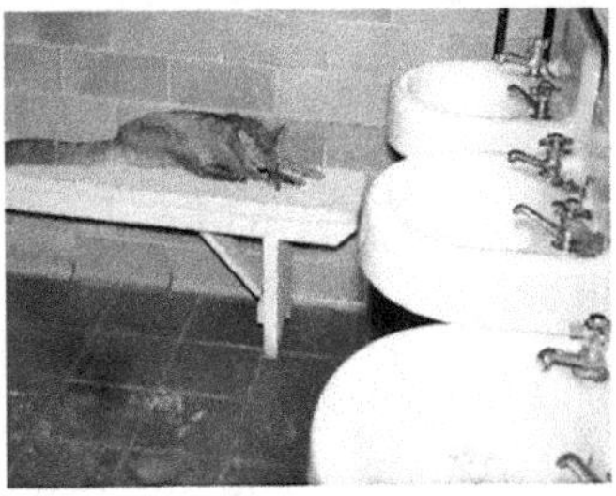

Bathroom facilities were in an adjacent hut laid out with toilets in open stalls, community urinals, sinks, and a community shower room. You never knew what you might find there in the morning. Wild-life was plentiful.

The mess hall was down the street. The camp was named for William P Upshur (1881-1943) who was awarded the Congressional Medal of Honor in 1915 for action in Haiti.

THE 1956 ARAB ISRAELI WAR

In July 1956 "Nasser grabbed the canal" – the Suez; Egypt "nationalized" it. This made the front pages and we all knew about it. However, we did not know much of its background or anything that followed. We were too busy becoming Marines. The Suez Canal, built by the French and opposed by the British, had opened for business on 17 November 1869. On 10 May of the same year, the U.S. Transcontinental Railroad opened. These two events shortened around the world travel time. Jules Verne's *Around the World in 80 Days* predicted it. **Nellie Bly**, pen name of investigative journalist, industrialist and inventor (55 gal. oil drum), **Elizabeth Jane Cochrane** (1864-1922) proved it in 72 days, 6 hours, 11 minutes and14 seconds in 1889-90. [45] No book on the military is complete without a "pin-up."

Britain bought a 44% interest in the canal by purchasing defunct Egyptian canal bonds in 1875.

Because of uncertain payments by the Ottoman Empire, the Ottoman Public Debt Administration was formed in 1881. The OPDA took over tax collections and financing infrastructure in the Ottoman Empire to insure full repayment of all debts; its final payment occurred on 25 May, 1954. [46]

Whether this had anything to do with Egypt's decision to "nationalize" the canal in 1956 is conjectural. In 1882 Britain invaded Egypt and took control of the canal, but by 1936 had pulled out most of its troops while keeping the Suez Zone. It had great strategic importance during the Boer Wars (1880-1 & 1899-1902) World War I (1914-18), and World War II (1939-45). Hitler's efforts to seize it with the Afrika Korp (1941- 43) under Rommel almost succeeded, but failed for lack of logistical support and the start of the War against the USSR.

In 1949 under UN decree, Israel became a Jewish State occupying "Palestine." This would not likely have succeeded had it not been for a 100 year pause in the Thirteen-hundred Years' War and the Jewish Holocaust. From 1856 until its collapse in 1923 The Ottoman Empire had been the "sick man of Europe."

In 1956 the war that had remained quiescent for 100 years after 1236 years of fighting was reignited when. Gamal Abdel Nasser seized the Suez, armed Jordanian, Palestinian Fedayeen Terrorists, and blockaded Israeli shipping from the straits of Tiran (entry way to the Gulf of Aqaba) and the Suez Canal. All was done with Soviet "encouragement."

The first modern knight and Nobel Peace Laureate rose to assist this cause, **Mohammed Yasser Abdel Rahman Abdel Raouf Arafat al-Qudwa** (1929-2004). Since Suez had been under the "protection" of the British and French, these two allies were infuriated by the blockade and threatened military action. President Eisenhower told them to "cool it." They eventually did, but not without a fuss. In the meanwhile the Fedayeen began terrorist raids against Israel. Terrorism has increased ever since.

Yasser Arafat

Although the UN urged peace, the emboldened President Nasser said, "No!" on 14 October 1956 and on 25 October signed a tri-partite agreement with Syria and Jordan placing all their armies under Egyptian command. Egypt and Syria eventually became the United Arab Republic (1958-61).

France had become friendly with Israel, and encouraged her with British agreement to attack Egypt. Israel would land paratroopers near the Canal and move an armored column across the Sinai. At the same time Britain and France would call for both Egypt and Israel to cease operations. Egypt would, "Of Course," refuse giving France and Britain an excuse to move in with their military to "protect" the canal. [47] The plan worked for a time.

On 29 October 1956 General Moshe Dayan launched the 6-day war during which Israel took Gaza, the Sharm el Sheikh (approaches to the Gulf of Aqaba), and much of the Saini Peninsula. On 31 October British and French air struck Egyptian air-fields near the Suez. By 5 November Israeli armor had punched its way across the Saini clearing out all Egyptian resistance while British and French paratroopers took Port Said, the northern entry point of the Suez Canal on the Mediterranean, but Egypt blocked the canal to all shipping.

A US sponsored resolution in the U.N. demanded a cease fire and the Soviets promised to use "*every kind of modern destructive weapon*" in their arsenal to stop the war – that meant tactical nukes. The U.S. promised to cut off all aid to Israel, if the fighting did not stop, but guaranteed another $1 billion from the International Monetary Fund if Israel pulled back.

On 7 November all fighting ceased with agreement of Israel and Great Britain. France objected. For once the U.S. joined with the Soviets despite its active brutal suppression of the Hungarian revolution from 4-10 November 1956. They insisted that the Canal go back to Egypt and that all French, British and Israeli troops be removed from conquered territories.

Troops were removed and the U.N. occupied the Sharm el Sheikh to permit Israeli access to Aqaba. This did nothing to interrupt the tripartite agreement between Egypt, Syria and Jordan or discourage Soviet aid to these countries. In the meanwhile, the CIA under Allen Dulles, brother of John Foster Dulles, Secretary of State, reported the dangers of Communist influence in Syria and began planning a *coup* code named "Wappen." In 1956 the CIA operated with minimal supervision, "*unmanaged by the White House and unsupervised by Congress*" despite the Bruce-Lovett report's finding that the agency had a "*penchant for creating political mayhem around the globe.*" [48]

OPERATION WAPPEN PHASE I

Operation Wappen was the brain child of **Kermit Roosevelt Jr. (1916–2000)**, grand-son of "Teddy" Roosevelt. A British Defector to the Soviets, Kim Philby described him, "*He was a courteous, soft-spoken Easterner with impeccable social connections, well-educated rather than intellectual, pleasant and unassuming as host and guest. An equally nice wife. In fact, the last person you would expect to be up to his neck in dirty tricks.*" [49] The maternal side of his father's family suffered with depression, alcoholism and bipolar disease. Like his father who was a brilliant linguist who served in military intelligence, [50] he was a shadowy James Bond, super-spy type who would later be responsible for the coup re-establishing Mohammad Reza Pahlavi as Shah of Iran from 1967-1979. "Wappen," (pronounced "*Vappen*") a Germanic word meaning a "coat of arms or shield," is not to be confused with "Waffen" meaning "armed."

During this era, President Eisenhower seemed to be overawed by his Ivy League staff. As a result, his Secretary of State, John Foster Dulles (1888-1959) Princeton, and his brother, Allen Dulles (1893-1969) also Princeton, seemed to have free rein to scheme almost anything. [51]

From 1800 to 1960, real analytical history was taught. This bears no resemblance to what most public schools and even universities in much of the world teach today. They teach "social studies" a "revisionist" or "class struggle" brand of history along with "political correctness" described in Part II of the *Manifesto of the Communist Party.* Many of that bygone era understood the difference between secular and orthodox Islamic states. They understood Kipling's Ballad of East and West where ***"never the twain shall meet."*** [52]

Despite common beliefs, our God is not the same as Islam's. [53] Allah is a determinist god, responsible for both good and evil in the world. [54] They studied the *Korân* so as to learn how the leaders of Islamic countries thought. In the dying days of the Ottoman Empire a movement known as the "Young Turks" began. They were "secularists," mostly children of the Turkish elite or "intelligentsia" who had gone to universities in Christian Western Europe.

They liked the freedom and modern advancements. There was a different attitude toward women who were not to be inferior to men in marriage, but an "ezer" or "savior / deliverer" of their husbands. [55] This was the Judeo-Christian concept of a "help meet" (Gen 2:18-20). The potential favoritism and jealousies of the harem and polygamy were absent. The concept of vengeance, "an eye for an eye," the *lex talionis* of the Semitic Hammurabi's Code, is a matter of doctrine in the *Korân*, (2:178, 194; 5:45) but was discouraged in Christian society (Matt 5:38-41). It led to the chaos of *blood feuds* and *honor killings* among Ottoman families, clans, tribes and principalities. In the West there was an attitude of free thought. Men could change their minds or "repent" in religious terms. Orthodox Islam believed in a different god. Man had little choice. [56]

Christian thought laid the blame for evil on mankind. Man had the will to choose; he had "free will." Natural law was also part of God's universe where sun and rain came to both just and unjust. (Matt 5:45). Parliaments ruled in the West. The differences between Biblical Judaism and Christianity are found in the Sermon on the Mount (Matt 5-7) and in Christ's parables and teachings. In Islam, man's behavior was predestined by God. God even used rain and wind to punish man. Eve was sinful and both she and Adam were "thrown out" of the idyllic Garden of Eden (*Korân* 64:14).[57] For that matter, Eve's name is not mentioned in the *Korân*. This event was not seen as an "opportunity" for advancement to "*become as one of us*" portrayed in Judeo-Christian doctrine (Gen 3:20-24).

In the Ottoman Empire Sultans and viziers ruled with an iron fist and a "silken cord," [58] often under the watchful eye of imams. These beliefs came from the *Korân*, especially from the more militant chapters written when the prophet lived in Medina. [59] Much doctrine in the more peaceful Mecca chapters was abolished or "abrogated" (*Korân* 2:106).

Definitions of War and Peace were not the same as in the West. War existed where Sharia was not; peace was where it was; it has nothing to do with conflict. [60] Negotiation with unbelievers is also not possible (*Korân* 9:7, 17, 28). [61] Imams prevented printing in the Ottoman Empire until the 18th Century and then only for non-religious books. [62] They prevented teaching artillery methods in the army. Modern banking with money lending was prohibited under Sharia Law. Demi-people (Christians and Jews) had to do it.

Lending was discouraged among Jews, but permitted for Christians (Matt 25:27). Only the "Auspicious Incident," the destruction of the Janissaries in 1826 led to needed military reforms. [63] A new Constitution (1876-8) brought 2 years of parliamentary government, but Imams opposed and got it abolished. Despite this setback, the Young Turks managed to continue to modernize the Empire with ports, canals, railroads, sanitary sewer systems, public water supplies, secular education, and the Sultans' opulent life-style. All cost money increasing the public debt and religious opposition. By 1880 Ottoman public debt reached a point causing British, French and German financial interests to take over the Ottoman treasury and taxation in an effort to collect it. [64]

Mustafa Kemal Ataturk

In 1908 constitutional government returned to stay. The carnage of World War I and Turkish War that followed led to the rise of **Mustafa Kemal Atatürk** (1881-1938) and the victory of secularism and the Young Turks.

Islamic fundamentalism and secularism has gone in cycles since the 7th Century with imams on the side of the "true believers" and their strict interpretation of the *Korân*. Turkey's secularism was opposed by many imams. This led to the establishment of the Sunni Muslim Brotherhood, founded by **Hassan al-Banna** (1906 -1949) of Egypt in 1928. Its purpose was to bring back, the Caliphate, in an Islamic Ottoman Empire as a strict Islamic state. One of their many spin-offs was Al-Qaida. Both espoused the methods of Muhammad ibn Abd al-Wahhab (1703-1792) who was a Sunni and strict follower of the *Korân*. He used terror methods outlined in the *Korân* to persuade more secular Muslims to become "true believers" (*Korân* 5:33; 9:5; 33:61). Sharia law, outlined in mostly the Medina chapters of the *Korân,* [65] would be the law of the land, not Western laws. Although not popular in his time Wahhab had become the imam to the House of Saud, that now controls Saudi-Arabia. With its oil dividends the

Hassan al-Banna

Saudis steadily purchased western oil interests and by 1970 oil money began pouring into the "Kingdom." The Muslim Brotherhood and Al-Qaida benefited from various Saudi sources.

Following the Suez fiasco of 1956 President Eisenhower and the newly elected (10 Jan 1957), "Conservative," British Prime Minister Macmillan feared Soviet support of the developing Egyptian, Syrian, Jordanian combine. It would weaken Western influence in the region and threaten oil (energy) supplies to the West. The Soviet leaning Syrian government had to go. The British MI6 under Sir Dick Goldsmith White, KCMG, KBE (1906-1993) and the U.S. CIA under the guidance of **Allen Dulles (1893-1969)** and Kermit Roosevelt planned a joint operation and Wappen was born.[66] Its first phase was also known as Operation Straggle. It would bring down the Syrian government with bribery ending the Egyptian tri-partite agreement. Selected Syrian Military officers were paid $3 million in bribes to go along with a "regime change." They took the money, exposed the plot, and US officers in Syria, Col. Robert W. Molloy (Army Attaché), Francis J. Jeton and Howard E. Stone (alleged CIA agents) were deported. Allen's brother, John Foster Dulles at State denied responsibility, expelled the Syrian ambassador to the U.S. withdrew the US ambassador from Syria, declared Syria a "Soviet satellite," and imposed economic sanctions. There were allegations that Syria had received 123 MIGs; these proved false. However, "if at first you don't succeed, …." So the British MI6 and CIA began plotting another coup. This time it would involve assassination and invasion by U.S. Marines. [67] We knew none of this.

QUANTICO

"This map shows no stream here!!"

The Marine Corps Base at Quantico Virginia is large. It extends from the Potomac River northeast into the Virginia countryside. It is hilly, heavily forested and crisscrossed with firebreaks often containing power lines.

MARINE CORPS SCHOOLS QUANTICO

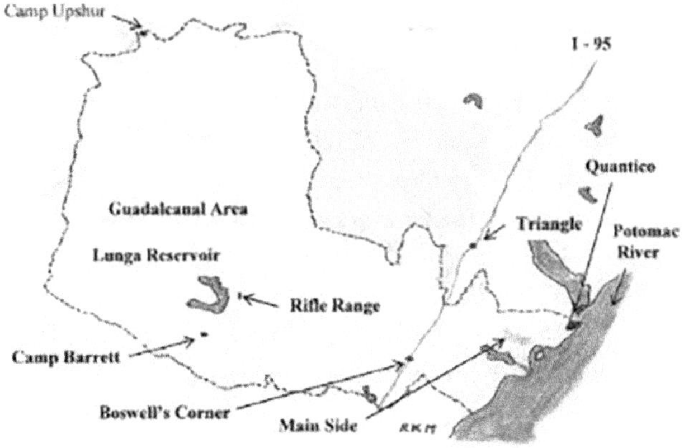

It was moved to Camp Barrett (mid lower left). Lunga Reservoir, named for a river and point of land on Guadalcanal, included a large heavy weapons impact area and could also serve as a practice area for amphibious landings. Main Side (lower right) was where most administrative buildings, the Officer's Club and FBI training area were located.

Outdoor class in the rain

Being a Marine is an all- weather occupation. The climate was humid varying from 70% to 90%. You sweat in summer and froze in winter. In July / August the average high temperatures were 88-86°F. From December to February the average lows were 31-26°F. The average rainfall was 39" per year and snowfall 16" per year. We had no air conditioning, but the huts were warm during the winter. Clothing was put on or removed so long as we were in uniform – usually combat dress. Training prepared us well for what we were to face; it was a mixture of class room and field combat exercises. Target practice was with the M-1 Garand 0.30 cal. rifle and 0.45 cal. M 1911 pistol. We were familiar with grenades, .30 cal. machine guns (air and water cooled) plus the **Browning automatic Rifle (BAR)**. In artillery training we fired 105 mm howitzers. All in our Basic Class qualified at least as Marksmen with the rifle. We were told this was the first time it had ever happened. I was a marksman with the rifle and sharpshooter with the pistol. There were plenty of "Experts" with both.

Physical Fitness was a must. It included the obstacle course, **rope lines across streams and gullies. A few got wet.**

Marches were long (15-20 miles) always with full packs and combat gear and occasionally all night. Much of it involved arduous physical activity in foul fall and winter weather. It was just what the Marine Corps wanted. When it rained, "***It was a great day for the attack.***" We were also learning Murphy's Laws of Combat. ***The worse the weather, the more you are required to be out in it. No matter which way you have to march, it's always uphill.*** [68] My being unmarried was also by design. "***If the Marine Corps wanted you to have a wife, they will issue you one.***"

Despite Hungary and the Middle East our training lasted 32 weeks as planned. By February 1957, the Virginia winter and our training were over. We had made the transition from "fat, dumb, and happy," to a "lean, mean, Marine Corps fighting machine" and were told to choose our military occupational specialties (MOS). I was courted for a time by Marine Air and was tempted. However, I would have to change my reserve commission to "regular" and extend my contract by 4 years. By this time I was firmly committed to a medical career, so did not accept the offer. Our five married lawyers in H Company would certainly go to the Judge Advocate General School upon graduation from Basic School. All selected JAG School and the lawyer MOS. I kept quiet about medical school and selected guided missiles (0702), artillery (0802), and armor (1802). Those specialties had bigger guns, better food and vehicles for transportation.

The fact that all these were prime targets on anyone's battlefield hadn't entered my mind. Having escaped "sea duty" by selecting the Marine Corps option in college, I was interested in combat arms with **less "ground pounding"** and better "*rations.*"

On 12 February 1957 we received our orders. I reported to the Commandant Marine Corps Schools, Quantico for the Basic Artillery Orientation Course (0802) for 4 weeks. Several of our lawyers got 0302 (infantry) and at least one ended up as (0802). In the service you never anticipate anything, "***In the beginning was the word and the word did change!***"

The evening before our graduation parade, when we got to march to *Semper Fidelis* and the *Marine Corps Hymn* in front of General Twining and other top brass at Basic School, we were invited to the traditional "Mess Night." This was a banquet attended by all officers in dress blues. At each table of eight there was one of our top instructors at Basic School. Lt. Colonel **Joseph Ronald "Bull" Fisher** (1921-1981) ate with us. [69]

In Korea he was "Chesty" Puller's right hand man and one of "the Chosin few;" with a Navy Cross to prove it. During the night of 25 November 1950 on "East Hill" overlooking Hagaru-ri and the main supply route to Marine Corps positions, with orders to "hold it at all costs," 1st Lt. "Bull" Fisher, then company commander of "I" company, held off what must have been a regimental sized Chinese Army attack. It was done during the coldest Korean winter in 100 years; temperatures dropped to minus 35°F. The ground froze solid, medical supplies froze, lubricants gelled, batteries died, and many guns wouldn't work. "I" Company had 3 machine guns, a few mortars and their hand held weapons. It came down to "rifle butts and bayonets." By morning the assault had been broken and an estimated 700 Chinese were dead on the hill and within their position. When Col. Chesty Puller asked for a body count, Fisher reported, "A whole piss pot full!" to which Puller replied that he was "glad that he had at least one officer who could count accurately."[70] Probably the greatest compliment to be paid to the Chosin Few came from Chairman Mao Zedong in orders to Chinese General Song Shilun:

"*The American Marine First Division has the highest combat effectiveness in the American armed forces. It seems not enough for our four divisions to surround and annihilate its two regiments. (You) should have one or two more divisions as a reserve force.*"[71]

After dinner we sat with him while he answered our questions about the Corps. Finally he said, "***Men, There is something you've got to know. If we fight another political war like Korea, it will ruin the morale of the U.S. Armed Forces for a generation.***"

What he meant was a war governed by politically driven "rules of engagement." He was right; it took us a generation to get over Vietnam. In my opinion, politicians should not micromanage or impose political solutions on the military during combat operations. They should leave that to the generals they have appointed to lead the armed services. Even in war, Christianity has a civilizing influence on individuals. (Deut 20 all; 21:10-14)

Artillery School was conducted by Major "Scream'n Willie" Willis L. Gore (1923-2004). He was also a veteran of the Chosin Reservoir Campaign (27 Nov – 13 Dec 1950) and up to that time was allegedly the last artillery commander in the U.S. armed services history to order direct artillery fire with canister. Canister shot [72] was a round commonly used in the Civil War in "direct fire" against massed troops.

Chosin was one of the Marine Corps' celebrated battles along with Belleau Wood, Guadalcanal, and Iwo Jima. It involved an organized retreat along 78 miles of roadway between hills from the Chosin Reservoir (Yudam-ni, Singhun-ni & Hagaru-ri) to the port of Hungnam on North Korea's east coast. It was fought against a Chinese Army that surrounded them with 2 to 1 odds in their favor. The 1st Marine Division and elements of the US Army's 3rd and 7th Infantry had other ideas.

It was fought in snowy minus 40°F weather. Many walked and fought on frost bitten feet and persevered. They took heavy casualties, but inflicted even worse and got away intact. [73] The Chinese used massed troop formations in human waves. The story goes that when Gore's unit ran out of standard artillery rounds, his men dug gravel from the roadway, shoveled it into the mouths of their 105 mm howitzers. Gore used left over cut powder charges in rehabilitated spent casings to fire gravel at the enemy. "***If you run out of ammo, throw rocks at 'em and hit 'em with shovels.***" The following is an online posting that confirms this sort of activity by artillery on the way out of the Chosin Reservoir.

"***Knew a guy that witnessed these human wave attacks. He said they'd cram 105's full of barbed wire, ball bearings, rocks or anything else they could get their hands on. Then lowered the guns and fire. They'd cut one wave of Chinese to bits. The next wave would advance, pick up the weapons from the dead as many were unarmed then charge.***" [74]

The Marines had one major advantage in the fight – air superiority that bombed the Chinese troop concentrations with napalm during the day in the surrounding hills. Casualties on the Chinese side were horrible: U.S. lost 1,029 killed, 4894 missing (mostly dead), 4582 wounded, 7338 non battle casualties – mostly frost bite. The Chinese suffered 19,202 killed and 28,954 non-battle casualties – unofficial estimation was 60,000. [75]

Major Gore taught us many tricks of the trade including how to attach gun trails to trucks so as to go into action within 30-60 seconds. We were also introduced to the 106-5 mm recoilless rifle "reckless-rifle" that was portable and tripod mounted, as well as a newer device, the **Ontos** (Greek for "the thing" and also the title of a 1951 science-fiction horror thriller). It was a "light" 9 ton tracked vehicle that carried 6 of these things. Its official name was, "**Rifle, Multiple 106 mm Self-propelled, M50.**"

The 106 mm recoilless rifles also fired 105 mm shells. When it was first tested by the Army the back blast from all six rifles fired simultaneously blew the brick facade off a nearby building and blew out windshields of nearby staff cars. The Army cancelled its order. The Marines didn't; it looked like a pretty good "thing" for us jar-heads.

We had them at Operation Deep Water, but they were sent home before Wappen. [76] Recoilless guns were invented before WWI and saw limited action in WWII in the hands of Soviet troops against the Germans as tank killers.

The Marine Corps found the Ontos very useful in Vietnam as a direct fire anti-personnel weapon. However, they were withdrawn from service in 1969. 105 mm recoilless rifles are mostly used by the U.S. Forest Service today in shooting down avalanches at ski resorts. [77]

Towards the end of our training we had the opportunity to observe an impressive show of heavy weapons. This included artillery, tanks and close air support runs with live ammunition. This is a **flame throwing tank** at Lunga Reservoir.

CAMP LEJEUNE, F-2-10, & "OPERATIONS DEEP WATER & WAPPEN"

On 1 May 1957 I reported for duty to the commanding officer of the 10th Marines at Camp Lejeune, North Carolina and was assigned to India Battery, 3rd Battalion, 10th Marine Regiment (I-3-10) for continued "on the job training." Work days were long with little time off. We practiced artillery with and without live fire.

The junior officers in the battery stood a rotational officer of the day duty in which the gun park, mess halls, barracks and other properties were inspected and protected during the night. We even chased a few alligators out of the gun park. At the time our principal armaments were the **105 mm howitzer** and **4.2 inch mortar.**

"***Don't ever be the first, don't ever be the last and don't ever volunteer.***"
Murphy

In June 1957 a call went out for volunteers for a special mission to the Mediterranean Sea – "Operation Deep Water." The regular Med Battalion was already on station. Their tour of duty was 6 months; this trip would be shorter. Going to "the Med" was considered great duty since you could visit various ports that usually included Barcelona, Caen, Athens and other tourist places. "The word" that often changed was that "nothing much was happening out there." So I volunteered, disobeying Murphy.

Although still "administratively" in India Battery, I was sent immediately, without official orders, to Fox Battery (F-2-10). Orders would not come for "administrative purposes" until 25 August 1957 just before our departure. All this irregular "administrative stuff" should have warned me that "something foul was a-foot," but I was still new to this business. Troops from all over the 2nd Marine Division were similarly transferred into the 6th Marine Regiment leaving many units seriously shorthanded. There was also a sudden change in leadership of the 6th Regiment. Col. Austin C. "shifty" Shofner, a Marines' Marine and combat hero from World War II, became Regimental C.O.

Captain Cain was my new skipper. He had enlisted in WWII, received a battlefield commission in Korea and had extensive combat artillery fire control experience from his service in the "Iron Triangle." [78] He knew the Marine Corps inside out and backwards from an enlisted as well as a company officer's perspective. He made sure that his young officers worked closely with enlisted ranks. The Marine Corps had ordered all "mustangs" (officers promoted from the ranks) to either obtain a college degree or leave the service. Captain Cain had just finished his degree from the University of Maryland Extension Service. This had required sacrifice and effort, but such was the devotion of many officers in The Corps.

In my first interview with Captain Cain, he told me that he knew from India Battery about my ability to get shells on target and that on the upcoming operation I would be in charge of the forward observer teams and be attached to the infantry of 3rd Battalion, 6th Marines.

When I was growing up, my parents took an annual trout fishing vacation in Idaho's **Sawtooth Mountains.** [79] At the time my father was stationed at Public Health Service hospitals in Cleveland OH, Norfolk VA, and Chicago, IL. From 1943 to 1945 he was at the US Maritime Training Station, Sheepshead Bay, Brooklyn, NY as Commanding Officer, Hospital Corps School. Auto trips took 3 to 4 days.

Highways were mostly paved and two lanes. Unlike the Interstates today, they followed the contour of the land. Before World War II, US Highway 30, which we followed to Twin Falls, ID, where my maternal grandparents lived, had a 100 mile stretch of gravel in western Nebraska.

One of our car-games was for each to estimate the distance between the top of one hill to the next; I got very good at it.

My accuracy became even more acute in my teen years when I worked with my grandfather, **John E Hayes** (1877-1962)[80] doing long distance land surveys in southern Idaho during the summers from 1947 to 1952. This taught me skill in estimating distances and checking them against reality. This later allowed me to move artillery "fire for effect" quickly from an initial burst from the "base piece" to the target with often only one test round.

His example as well as my father's instilled within me a love of country and the desire to serve it. I have spoken of my father's service in the U.S. Public Health Service. My grandfather was responsible for building many water projects in the western United States starting with the Twin Falls Project in 1903. A little known incident in his life included direct war-time service. He had wanted to serve in the Army during World War I, but was rejected because he was too old. At the outbreak of World War II he wrote the War Department, now called The Department of Defense, offering to be of service in any capacity they desired. About midway into 1942 he received a call from the War Department asking if he was serious. He said yes and they asked if he would help them build an airport. This was how he became the chief engineer in the construction of the Wendover, Utah airfield. He did not know the purpose of it at the time except that it was "ultra-secret." It turned out to be where the pilots were trained who dropped the atom bombs on Japan to end World War II.[81]

During this first interview Captain Cain also advised me to purchase my own **.45 cal. M1911 Automatic pistol**. If things "got ugly," I would need reliable self-protection. The Captain knew Murphy's Combat Laws: "***Never forget your weapon was made by the lowest bidder.***" The usual Marine Corps issue pistol was often difficult to use. The trigger pull was frequently hard, up to 15 lbs. A 3 pound pull made them much handier. He told me to get a pistol as soon and inexpensively as I could by mail order. This would give me a "receiver" with a valid serial number. I should take it to the armory and have it "match conditioned." I ordered one from "Golden State Arms" in California for $18 (#929790) and took it to the armory. It came back with almost all parts except the receiver replaced. I have it to this day and it is still pristine. It has never been fired in anger.

Since we would have no live fire exercises, my first assignment with F-2-10 was maintenance officer that included the motor pool and supply shed. My motor sergeant was an old salt who had been busted down from gunny sergeant (E-7) to sergeant (E-5) for some shenanigans in Okinawa. I will not go into the details, but Sgt. "Fixit" could get anything done he set his mind to. He was a *scrounger extraordinaire* who knew the ropes of the "midnight- supply depot."

Some of our equipment in the supply shed was either missing or in bad condition. This included several "dead-lined" vehicles in our motor pool. Both our 0.30 cal. machine-gun barrels were rusted out. There were no tools in any of our 3 tool boxes. In the next 6 weeks, all that and more was taken care of. We were in A-1 condition when we shipped out. I was staying close to the enlisted ranks and learning fast. We immediately went into intensive training.

Our first exercises were at the Amphib Base in Little Creek, Virginia. Here we practiced ship to shore landings. Operation Deep Water's purpose was to demonstrate a new concept, "Vertical Envelopment" to NATO General Officers. In 1947 planners in the Marine Corps realized the potential use of helicopters to land troops behind enemy lines and by-pass heavily defended beaches such as encountered at Omaha on D-Day, 6 June 1944. The first Marine helicopter squadron (HMX-1) was established 1 December 1947. In 1948 a platoon was lifted ship to shore. The Korean War (1950-53) proved the value of helicopters, especially in moving wounded troops from battlefield to MASH units, but the practical movement of large units would await the development of helicopters that could handle the job. By 1956 Marine Corps Schools at Quantico had fully developed this concept and had the helicopters to do it. All this was part of the Marine Corp's forward thinking that caused them to develop ship to shore amphibious landings for which they became famous during World War II.

This picture was taken at Quantico in 1956 landing 80 men using Sikorsky H-19 Chickasaws. Ours would be the first helicopter deployment of a fully intact battalion in support of an infantry regiment making a simultaneous amphibious beach assault 20 miles distant. During World War II glider and paratroops were used in a similar manner, but troops were scattered to such an extent that they could fight only as partisans or small units for several days. "Vertical envelopment" became a tactic used extensively by large and small units from the Vietnam era to the raid against Osama Bin Laden. We trained for this from an aircraft carrier off Morehead City. H-19s could carry only 8 men. A swarm was needed to move a battalion (700 men). We landed in the Cherry Point, NC area where we matched wits the 82nd Airborne Division, "aggressors" from Fort Bragg.

On August 21, 1957 Secretary of State, John Foster Dulles conferred with Admiral Andrew Radford and General Nathan Twining (USAF, Chairman of the Joint Chiefs of Staff) about Syria and Russian Communist influence in the Middle East. Dulles was "thinking of the possibility of "***fairly drastic action***." [82] We didn't know we were the "fairly drastic action."

We were a week from our departure date when the skipper made his final changes in our assignments. I was assigned as artillery liaison and forward observer with 11 men to compose 3 teams for 3rd Battalion 6th Marines (3-6).

Colonel **Austin C "Shifty" Shofner** (1916-1999), [83] a Marines' Marine, depicted here as a 1st Lt., our CO of troops, commanded the reinforced 6th Marine Regiment. He served with great distinction in World War II (Distinguished Service Cross and 2 silver stars). He survived the Bataan Death March following the fall of Corregidor. About a month later he and nine others overpowered guards, escaped into the Philippine jungles, joined remnants of the Philippine Army, and conducted guerilla raids against the Japanese. About a year later he was evacuated by submarine from Mindanao and assisted Mac Arthur's staff planning the invasion of the Philippines. He was promoted to brevet Major and commanded an Army battalion during the rest of the war. His battle awards included the DSC and Silver Star.

2nd Lt. James Benson would take my place as Maintenance Officer and 2nd Lt. Don Schaet, who was quick with math, would be in charge of the fire direction center. Calculations in those days were done by head, hand, and slide-rule. Captain Cain also told us that our battery would be "beefed up." Instead of six 105mm howitzers we would have eight.

Our 4.2" mortars would be increased from two to six. In addition two

8" 203 mm self-propelled howitzers, M 109s would join us from Force Troops in 29 Palms, California. I saw at least one Ontos operating with 3-6. It also

appeared in *Life Magazine*. At the time no one thought much about this, but we might have wondered why all these heavy weapons were being sent with us, especially when our ammunition was "blanks." That might impress the NATO brass with noise and smoke during Operation Deep Water, but would be worthless otherwise. With the Med Battalion already "on station" we would have nearly a Battalion of artillery fire power to support 6th Marine Regiment "reinforced."

"THE MED"

On the evening of the 29th of August we packed personal gear in our freshly stenciled **locker boxes**, loaded the trucks and lined them up.

On the 30th we "saddled up" and "moved out." About midafternoon we pulled up to a flat concrete quay in the Morehead City, NC harbor. My 11 man forward observer teams and I joined the 3rd Battalion, 6th Marines infantry. I was back with the "ground pounders" and going to sea. At least these ships wouldn't be "tin cans", destroyer escorts.

There were no ships in sight, but we were told to bed down after supper as best we could on the concrete slab. The transports would be there in the morning. On 31 August the **USS Olmsted APA 188,**[84] a Haskell Class 1944 WWII troop transport and the **USS Chilton**[85], a Bayfield Class 1942 vintage transport pulled up to the quay.

I boarded with 3-6, on the Olmsted. F-2-10 boarded the USS Chilton APA 38. Their landing would be from the sea. Ours would be from the air.

Heavy equipment would be aboard the **USS Fort Snelling LSD-30.**[86] We didn't know it at the time, but we were the first Marine Artillery unit to be deployed to the Mediterranean. [87]

The **Terrebonne Parish, LST 1156**[88] would carry many of our vehicles and other heavy cargo.

Operation Wappen was never mentioned and is not in Navy and Marine Corps official reports, although the trip to Souda Bay, Crete is. [89]

By 1 September 1957 we were underway. Our mission was clandestine from the start. As noted previously we were still at Camp Lejeune for "pay and administrative purposes" despite our being in "the field." As I learned many years later, our mission included Operation Wappen. This explained our "beefed up" artillery battery, reinforced infantry regiment, and all the secret "administrative" folderol. According to the published reports about 50 years later:

"***In September 1957, the US deployed a fleet to the Mediterranean, armed several of Syria's neighbors, and incited Turkey to deploy 50,000 troops to its border. Secretary of State John Foster Dulles suggested that the US sought to invoke the "Eisenhower Doctrine" of retaliating against provocations, and this intention was later confirmed in a military report. No Arab state would describe Syria as a provocateur, and these military deployments were withdrawn.***" [90]

On our first day at sea I found the Officer of the Deck Division, a Navy lieutenant. After consultation with my men I volunteered them for duty with the 40mm anti-aircraft batteries and the 5" gun. Taking care of and manning them meant chipping rust off the gun tubs and painting them with nice fresh "battleship gray." In return, my men would become part of "Ship's Company." They would get free run of the ship at all times, eat in the regular Navy mess and have Navy PX privileges. Ship's company had a better mess and PX. My men readily agreed to their new conditions. I was housed with the officers of 3-6 and Air-Ground officers from MAG-26, in "troop officers' country" on the main deck. We slept 3 deep in bunks. The troops slept 6 deep on fold down "racks" in "the hold."

Marine Troops were confined to quarters in "the hold" for all but several hours per day. They ate in the troops' mess and purchased at the troops' PX. This permitted ship's company to operate the vessel without obstruction or interference.

When troops were released most poured out onto the deck. They could be found getting some sun and lounging with their magazines and card games all over the ship.

During the cruise illness aboard the **USS Kleinsmith APD 134**, a high speed transport with minimal medical facilities and designed to land small combat groups (Marine Raiders, Army Rangers, and Navy UDTs and SEALS) on hostile beaches, transferred a sick man (see arrow) to the small hospital aboard the Olmsted.

On September 12 we passed through the **Straits of Gibraltar** heading into the Mediterranean.

We arrived at **Taranto, Italy** on 16 September 1957 for 3 days of liberty. Our convoy had been delayed by the LST 1156 that lost power and slowed us down. It arrived in Taranto a day later. Our trip across the Atlantic also included a major storm with 40' high waves and a trip through the Sargasso Sea.

OFFICER OF THE DECK

Taranto still had war damage; the town's Communist population was not pleased to see us. There were certain exceptions, however.

On our first day in port, I was assigned duty as Officer of the Deck. The men had been cooped up for 17 days and were eager to go ashore and blow off steam, but each would receive only 6 hours of liberty in two shifts per day, there being too many U.S. service men in the harbor for the Port Authorities to handle all at once.

My duty lasted 24 hours starting at 0800 on September 17. My post was at the gangway supervising those headed for liberty and later those returning. This exposed me to some of the more seamy side of service life. I had 4 Navy corps men to help me handle the more disorderly with shots of paraldehyde before being escorted to their bunks. After the last barge returned about midnight, I was permitted to get some rest, but was wakened about 0500 by the Navy deck officer who said I should come immediately to the gangway as the admiral's barge was approaching. When it came along side, the officer in charge delivered to me a Marine air-ground Major, in irons with a still soaking wet uniform, compliments of the fleet commander. He had been caught in the middle of the bay swimming back to the ship at 0200 allegedly having jumped into it to escape gun fire. I was ordered to take him to the brig and lock him up until his CO could verify the incident. Once there I got his irons off and got him a dry uniform. I don't know how it turned out except that the officer and his CO were ashore the next day looking for bullet holes in the pier from which he had allegedly escaped his assailants. By this time I had been accepted to Medical School to begin in 1958 and was interested in disease. I learned from the Corps Men that they had treated over 40 cases of GC and I saw my first and only positive microscopic dark-field examination for spirochetes.

During my liberty I accompanied one of the officers from 3-6 to a jeweler to get his watch repaired. He asked the clerk to mail it to him in

Caen, France, since we were scheduled to be there in several weeks. The clerk said he would mail it to us in Athens; we would be there, not in Caen. An argument ensued, but the officer received his watch in Athens.

Everybody out there seemed to know what we were doing and where we were going before we did. I was getting my first lesson in military "intelligence." On 19 September 1957 we departed Taranto. We never got to Caen.

THIRD BATTALION SIXTH MARINES

Turkey at the time was a staunch US ally and had fought with the U.S. during the Korean War. Unlike now, it was secular and Imams had little power. On 22 September 1957 we passed through the Dardanelles and approached Gelibolu (Gallipoli), Turkey (40°25'N, 26°40'E) from the south by way of the Sea of Marmara. Our camp was within sight of the Sea of Marmara. We were also near the old Turkish Headquarters during the Battle of Gallipoli. Our colonel, always vigilant, had us dig in as a rear echelon unit would do in a combat zone. We were spread out in unit areas, put up pup-tents and dug fox-holes, set up regular sentries and perimeter patrols. We would not have suffered as the Marines did in 1983 when 220 were killed in the Beirut Barracks bombing.

The Allied British landings in World War I took place on the tip of the Peninsula from the Mediterranean side. They might have been more successful had they landed in Thrace where we did in Operation Deep Water.

Unit patches noted here show **2-10**'s "Second to None" battalion patch at the top. F-2-10 (Fox Battery) was part of 2-10. The **10th Marine's** patch is on the left and **3-6's**, 3rd Battalion, 6th Marine's Battalion patch is on the right with its Presidential Unit Citation above for its action on Tarawa during WWII. My dog tags are in the middle. One for my body and the other for "graves registration" should that be necessary.

3-6 had a "reputation." It was known as "*Teufelhunden*" following the Battle of Belleau Wood (1-26 Jun 1918). The entire Marine Corps adopted its appellation, "Devil Dogs," from the name the Germans allegedly gave it. Its patch was the first ever used by a US expeditionary force.

It displayed a star with an Indian head in the middle. Brig. General John A Lejeune (1867 – 1942), commanded the 2nd Marine Division during World War I. He was known as "Old Indian." The single star represented Lejeune's rank in 1916. The black background mourned their dead comrades.

The background behind the star was yellow for the 1st Battalion, red for the 2nd Battalion, and blue (shown here) for the 3rd Battalion 6th Marines. 3-6 was also the first to be deployed during World War II when it was sent to Iceland (Danish territory) in May 1941 to prevent a potential German invasion. It was not brought home until February 1942. It participated late in the Guadalcanal Campaign and many other island campaigns in the South Pacific. [91]

When I served in 3-6, only bachelors could serve in that unit from Colonel to private. Every man, officers included, dug their own fox-hole. At the field kitchen officers ate last after the enlisted ranks in reverse order of rank – colonel last. "Esprit" was high.

OPERATION DEEP WATER

On 25 September we were airlifted by helicopter to our landing zone near Izzetiye, Turkey (40°49"N, 26°38'E) just off highway E-87 about 10 -15 miles inland north of the southern coast of Saros Gulf and about 28 miles due north of Gallipoli and 2 miles south of Keşan.

At the same time F-2-10 was landing via amphibious tractors (LVTs Amtracks) on the Turkish north coast of Saros Gulf.

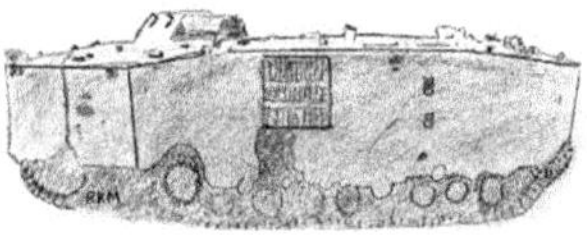

Depicted is an **LVTP-5**. It was armed with .30 cal. machine guns, was completely enclosed, and capable of carrying 34 troops. Another version, the LVTH6, available to us had a turret mounted 105 mm howitzer.

I remember our practice landings at Little Creek using the 5s. At first it was frightening. When we dropped out of the LST's (landing ship tank) bow door, the tractor sank about 10 feet below the surface then slowly came back up to the point that its top deck was awash. The gun turret was out of water and the crew could open the hatches and come out if necessary. We traveled about 10 mph in water towards the shore. These were fantastic devices. We were protected by steel armor and water surrounding us. The tractor was also maneuverable and presented a very poor target silhouette in the water. It was capable of about 30 mph on land. Exit was from the rear. It was the forerunner of all modern armored personnel carriers.

Operation Deep Water Map

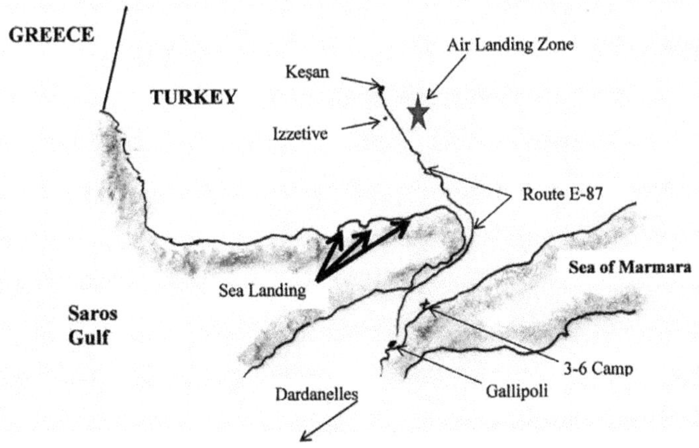

From our hill side we faced west and overlooked a two lane highway, E-87, and a wide valley. Attempts to contact the cruiser 20 to 30 miles away in Saros Gulf with our PRC-9 radios failed In accordance with Murphy's Law: "***Radios will fail as soon as you need fire support desperately.***" However, we could listen to taxi radio traffic in Atlanta GA.

On 29 September, with Deep Water over, we moved to the beach, boarded the Olmsted and headed for Athens. The demonstration had been a success and without casualties. We arrived in **Piraeus, the port of Athens**, on 30 Sep 1957.

LIBERTY IN ATHENS

The Chilton is in the foreground and The USS Lake Champlain CVS-39 on the left in the background.

As a child and young teenager I had always wanted to visit Athens and see the "ruins" of Ancient Greece. I went sightseeing and was not disappointed. The **Acropolis** and Parthenon were all that I expected. Three years after the sack of Constantinople Athens fell in 1456 without resistance to the Ottoman Empire. The Parthenon was converted to a Mosque.

In 1687 a Venetian expeditionary force attempted to retake Athens. During the conflict, the Muslims stored gunpowder in the **Parthenon**. A Venetian shell fired at Turkish defenders on the Acropolis, hit the Parthenon, the powder exploded blowing the roof off and causing extensive damage. Ottoman occupation of Greece continued until 1821. An extensive restoration will not be completed until 2020. [92]

Meanwhile at the White House in Washington events were unfolding that would affect us. [93] Those attending meetings give a good idea about what might have been discussed. On 1 October *"In God We Trust"* appeared for the first time on our paper money. We went off any pretext of a precious metal standard in 1964, a violation of Constitution Article 1, Sections 8 & 10.

That evening President Eisenhower attended a party at the home of Secretary of State, John Foster Dulles. Allen Dulles, his brother, chief of the CIA, was also there. The day's appointments did not seem to have much to do with military matters.

In the morning of 2 October there was a 2 hour meeting of the National Security Council that included the President, Vice President Nixon, John Foster Dulles (Sec. of State), "Engine Charlie" Wilson (Defense Secretary), Gordon Gray (Office of Defense Mobilization), Robert Anderson (Deputy Sec. of Defense), Percival Brundage (OMB), Harold Stassen (Special Assistant for Disarmament), DA Fitzgerald (**International Cooperation Administration**), Arthur Larsen (Speech Writer), Raymond J Saulnier (Chairman Council of Economic Advisers), Christian A Herter (Under Sec. of State), Walter S Robertson (Asst. Sec. of State Far Eastern), James P Richards (**Special Assist, Middle Eastern Affairs**)

Gen Nathan F Twining (**Chairman Joint Chiefs of Staff**), Allen Dulles (**CIA**). Sherman Adams (Chief of Staff), Robert Cutler (National Security Advisor), Frederick M Dearborn (**Operations Coordinating Board – Defense Dept. & CIA**), Brig Gen. Andrew J Goodpaster (Staff Sec. to President and Liaison Officer of the Dept. of Defense), Donald Quarles (Deputy Sec. of Defense) G Frederick Reinhardt (**Counselor to State Dept. – Middle East**), Maurice Stans (Deputy Director Bureau of Budget – OMB), Mansfield Sprague (Assist. Sec of Defense for **International**

Security Affairs), James S Lay Jr. (**National Security Council**), Everett Gleason (**NSC – Security Analyst**).

Considering those in attendance, this meeting may have included discussions about international and special military operations in the Middle East.

On 3 Oct Willy Brandt was elected mayor of West Berlin. A press conference was held from 10:30-11:00. Earlier meetings had to do with this. On October 4, 5, 6, and 7 there were few meetings. On October 4 the big news was the launching of the Soviet's Sputnik, the first satellite in space.

On 6 October the Soviets conducted a nuclear test at Novaya Zemlya, USSR. The Asian flu reached Athens by 7 October and a third of us came down with a short-lived flu with gastroenteritis that caused many to stay close to the ship and modern plumbing.

Back home Time and Life Magazines reported on Operation Deep Water:

"Tardily but impressively, a simulated mushroom cloud rose over the coastal hills of Thracian Turkey. Huge amphibious tanks churned up golden Aegean beaches, and troop-laden helicopters scissored down out of azure Mediterranean skies. Then 8,000 U.S. Marines who had come 6,000 miles from Virginia (error: we came from NC***) in four weeks, landed in Turkey last week to grab a stake of ground just north of the historic shores of Gallipoli. The tactical problem set for NATO's Operation Deep Water was to assume that Turkey had been invaded from the north …***"

In the same issues of Time & Life was the story of Eisenhower's breaking Little Rock, Arkansas school segregation with the 101st Airborne Division. On October 8 Turkish and Syrian border guards exchanged fire. I later learned that Turkey was supposed to start an incident that was to signal the beginning of Operation Wappen. Both countries were conducting military maneuvers on their border.

Between 8:37-9:17 a White House meeting without title included Donald Quarles (Deputy Sec. of Defense), William M Holaday (Deputy Assist. Sec Defense, research and Development), Dr. John P Hagan (Vanguard Space Program), Sherman Adams (Chief of Staff), Howard Pyle (Aid to the President), Bryce Harlow (Congressional Liaison). This meeting almost certainly had to do with Sputnik and concern over the US space program. The rest of the day's meetings were individual and did not seem to involve military matters.

OPERATION WAPPEN

On 8 October, the USS Albany CA123 piped aboard its new skipper, Captain **John Sidney "Jack" McCain** Jr. (1911-1981). [94] He would be our flag officer on this mission, but ten years later he would be a full admiral, Commander in Chief of the Pacific Fleet and all forces in Viet Nam from 1968 to 1972. He was also the father of John S McCain III, who was a prisoner of War for 5 ½ years after being shot down and severely wounded over North Vietnam and who would later become Senator from Arizona and candidate for the Presidency of the U.S. [95] He and his father, also an admiral would have a guided missile destroyer named after them, the USS John S McCain.[96]

On 9 October our liberty was suddenly cancelled. We were not told why or of the previous day's fracas on the Turkish Syrian border or even about the change in command. We re-boarded our ships and sailed for Crete and Souda Bay and five days of conditioning marches in the White Mountains. We still knew nothing about a possible hostile landing in Syria. However, we discovered that our ships were being "combat loaded." Combat loading has serious implications. It is a logistical method to insure that what comes off a ship first is what is needed for combat first; last loaded is first out.

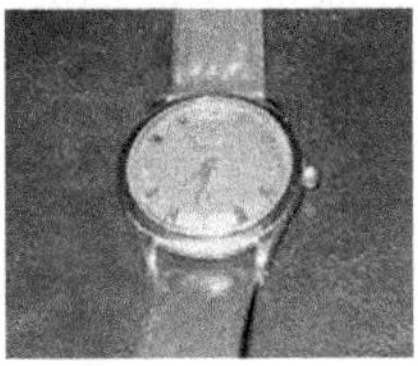

In preparation for a combat assignment, I purchased an Omega chronometer at the ship's store.

At the White House, Neil McElroy was sworn in as the new Secretary of Defense replacing Charles E Wilson. A number of military dignitaries briefly met from 8:23-8:37. It is unlikely that this meeting had anything to do with our situation.

However, from 9:00 to 10:55 AM there was a meeting of the National Security Council attended by the president and vice president, Christian Herter (Under Sec. of State), Neil McElroy (Sec. of Defense), Victor E Cooley (Dep. Dir. Office of Defense Mobilization), Fred C Scribner (Act. Sec of Treasury), Herbert Brownell (Atty. Gen), Percival Brundage (OMB), Harold Stassen (Mutual Security Administration – foreign aid), Brig. Gen. Alfred D Starbird (Chairman, Atomic Energy Commission), James H. Smith Jr. (US Agency for International Development), Arthur Larson (Director US Information Agency), Lewis E Berry (Act. Federal Civil Defense Administrator), Alan T Waterman (Director, National Science Foundation), J Wallace Joyce (National Science Foundation), William M Holaday (Spec. Jt. Assistant to Sec of Defense), John P Hagan (Director Project Vanguard), Detlov W Bronk (President National Academy of Sciences), Nathan F Twining (**Chairman, Joint Chiefs**), Allen Dulles (**Director CIA**), Sherman Adams (Chief of Staff), Wilton B Persons (Assist to President – Congressional Liaison), Robert Cutler (National Security Advisor), Clarence B Randall (Chairman of Council on Foreign Economic Policy) Brig Gen Andrew J Goodpaster (Defense Dept. Liaison Officer) AC Waggoner (Exec Assist to Mr. Holaday), Donald Quarles (Dep. Sec. of Defense), William Leonhart (Dept. of State), Maurice Stans (Bureau of Budget), Mansfield Sprague (Assist. Sec. of Defense for International Security Affairs), John Scoville (**CIA**), Frederick Dearborn (**Operations Coordinating Board – Dept. Defense & CIA**).

This meeting appears to have included several scientists and those involved with national security, international affairs, and secret operations. There may have been discussion about our situation and sputnik. As I found later, we were armed with nukes. Later that day the president met mostly one on one with Defense and State Department notables.

On 11 October a 2 hour Cabinet Meeting was held at the White House. It included most members of the Cabinet including those not engaged in military or clandestine affairs. On 12 October, 13 October and 14 October (Eisenhower's birthday), there were few meetings. On 15 October 1957 in the early PM our ships departed Souda Bay and headed for the Syrian Coast and Turkish border area.

At the time this photo was taken we had no knowledge of the future. It shows the junior officers of F-2-10 at **Souda Bay.** 2nd Lts. **RK Maddock** (left), **JW Benson** (middle), and **DE Schaet** (right).

As of this writing in 2015, Col. Donald Schaet, USMC (ret) is living in Georgia. James William Benson became a CPA in Atlanta and died in 2004. [97] In the background are the White Mountains of Crete.

We had heard in the news that John Foster Dulles denied that the US had any troops or serious intentions in the Eastern Mediterranean. We knew better, and so did the Russians. Rumors throughout the fleet were that several MIGs had been shot down. We were combat loaded and headed for a hostile beach. Little did we know how serious our situation was?

Meanwhile at the White House on 15 October a one hour meeting from10:58 – 11:55 AM with members of the Science Advisory Committee met with the President. The following were present: I.I. Rabi (**Professor of Physics, Columbia U**), LV Berkner (President of Assoc. of Universities, Inc.), HA Bethe (**Prof. of Physics , Cornell U**), DW Bronk (**President, National Academy of Sciences**), JB Fisk (**Exec VP, Bell Labs**), CP Haskens (Pres. Carnegie Institute of Washington), AG Hill (**Director of Research, Weapons Systems Evaluation Group**), JR Killian Jr. (**Pres. MIT**), EH Land (**Pres. Polaroid Corp.**), H Scoville Jr (**Air Force Scientific Advisory Board**), AT Waterman (**Director, National Science Foundation**), JB Weisner (**Director Research Laboratory of Aeronautics MIT**), JR Zacharias (**Prof Physics MIT**), Robert Cutler (National Security Advisor), Gen Andrew J Goodpaster (Defense Dept. Liaison Officer).

Immediately afterwards, a one on one meeting was held between Ike and John Foster Dulles (**Sec of State**) from 11:55 to 12:43. From what I know of meetings during this era, President Eisenhower rarely met one on one with anyone for more than 10 minutes. There were no further meetings that day. Those at the meeting were heavily weighted toward atomic physics and may have discussed our potential use of tactical nuclear weapons.

On **October 16** Queen Elizabeth was in Williamsburg, VA. She would arrive at the White House the next day, the day of our scheduled landing in Syria.

An "Off the Record" meeting was held between 8:50 and 9:11 AM. This would have been about 5 PM in the Eastern Mediterranean. Attending were Robert Cutler (**National Security Advisor**), Murray Snyder (Assist Sec. for Public Affairs Dept. of Defense), Frederick Dearborn (**Operations Coordinating Board – Defense Dept. & CIA**), Wilton Persons (Assist. To the President – Congressional Liaison), James Haggerty (Press Sec) and Brig Gen Andrew J Goodpaster (Defense Dept. Liaison Officer). This meeting likely concerned our potential landing and the use of nuclear weapons. A presidential decision was pending by this time.

At a pre-invasion briefing aboard the **USS Albany CA 123** [98] held about 5 PM on 16 October (about 9 AM in Washington), I was the most junior officer attending as artillery liaison with 3-6. Most were field-grade officers (Major to Colonel). At the end, there was a call for questions. No one seemed to have any, but I did and timidly raised my hand only partially. Colonel Shofner spotted me and said, "Yes, Lieutenant, what do you want to know?" "Sir," I said fearfully, "***What are we going to shoot at them? We have only blank ammunition and rumors have it that the closest ammo ship is 3 days distant.***" The Colonel responded pointing through a porthole towards the stern of the ship, "***Lieutenant, you see that sea-plane on the hook back there?" "Yes sir,***" I replied.

The Colonel continued, "***You'll be on that bird tomorrow morning at 0500 hours. You and the pilot will take off, and fly into Syria. When you spot the center of the Syrian Army, you will radio its map coordinates to the Navy and get the h— out'o there!!***" "***Yes Sir!***" I replied, "***but, Sir, what are we going to shoot at them?***" The Colonel, visibly uncomfortable, shuffled a bit, glanced down. "***We've got 50 nukes in the hold!***" I and everyone else in the room were frozen; we said no more and departed.

When I returned to the Olmsted, I asked the OD (Officer of the Deck) to waken me in the morning in time to make my rendezvous with the sea plane on the Albany.

Nuclear artillery [99] was fully developed and tested above ground in the Nevada Desert in 1953. In 1957 the M110 and M 115 howitzers were deployed capable of delivering a 203mm (8") W33 nuclear shell. It could yield 15 kilotons of destructive power. 80 of these shells were produced in 1952 and retired in 1957. These had about the same yield as the Hiroshima and Nagasaki bombs – 13-18 kt. with a fireball radius of about 0.13 to 0.15 miles. [100] About the same time a nuclear shell, the W48 capable of being fired from a 155 mm howitzer, was developed. Officially it went into production in 1963.

I wakened about 7:30 AM on 17 October (it was about 11:30 PM 16 Oct. in Washington). The ship was underway; I had not been called to get up earlier. I looked out the hatchway, the rising sun was to our stern and we were steaming at full speed westward. The Landing was off and we were headed for Palermo, Sicily where we arrived on 18 October. After 10 days in Palermo we went to Barcelona for 3 days then Gibraltar for 4 hours and then home. On 18 Nov 1957 we arrived safely in Morehead City.

On 17 October from 9:02 to 10:23 AM a National Security Council Meeting was held. Present were the President, Vice President , John Foster Dulles (Sec of State), Neil McElroy (Sec of Defense), Victor E Cooley (Office of Defense Mobilization), Robert Anderson (Sec. Treasury), Percival Brundage (OMB), Harold Stassen (Mutual Security Administration – foreign aid & Special Asst. for Disarmament), Lewis L Strauss (Chairman, Atomic Energy Commission),

James Smith Jr. (US Agency for International Development), Arthur Larson (Director US Information Agency), Gen Nathan F Twining (**Chairman, JCS**), Allen Dulles (**CIA**), Sherman Adams (Chief of Staff), Robert Cutler (Nat. Security Advisor), Frederick M Dearborn (**Operations Coordinating Board – Dept. Defense & CIA**), Clarence B Randall (Chairman of the Council on Foreign Economic Policy), Brig. Gen Andrew J Goodpaster (Defense Dept. Liaison Officer), Donald Quarles (Dep. Sec of Defense), Gerard Smith (Dept. of State), Frank Wisner (**CIA Directorate of Plans**), James S Lay Jr. (National Security Council), S Everett Gleason (NSC – Security Analyst). Almost anything involving military and foreign affairs was likely discussed. By this time we were on our way west and Wappen was off.

We received the **American Defense Medal** for our work.

F-2-10 distinguish itself in the artillery competition at Fort Bragg early in 1958. Captain Cain, battery commander received his instructions the morning of the competition. This included different firing positions over a two day period. Each artillery battery in the 10th Marine Regiment was to move 122 miles from Camp Lejeune to Fort Bragg to a designated position in the "impact area," set up, and hit a specified target. It would then move to the next position and repeat the process. I have forgotten the number of times we had to shoot and move, but it was considerable. The competition lasted two days. Captain Cain's reputation preceded him and from what we later heard, the CO of 10th Marine Regiment was watching us much of the time. I was the forward observer. When we arrived at our first firing position, I got very lucky. The target was an obsolete tank on top of a hill. The first round fired from the "base piece" landed about 50 yards short of the target. This was a golden opportunity to show off the skill of our battery. I sent the following orders back to the guns, "***Up five zero; high/low, time on target; fire for effect.***" An order to "fire for effect" "high/low time on target" meant that the 6 guns in the battery would fire their first round in a high angle trajectory. Then the guns would be lowered rapidly to a more flat trajectory and fire another 6 rounds timed so that all 12 rounds would hit the target simultaneously. This was commonly used in combat to make the enemy think that an entire battalion of artillery was shooting at them instead of just one battery or to saturate the target with double the rounds when firing at large numbers of massed troops. It happened that the shell from one of the guns firing at high angle plunged through the open hatch of the tank and the registration point disappeared in a tremendous explosion as all 12 rounds hit the target. We then packed up and moved to the next position. We completed our full schedule of moving and shooting different targets in one day with the least amount of ammunition, way ahead of the other batteries and won the competition. We were the "Fastest Guns in the East." 3-6 continued to distinguish itself in its further assignments. All of us 2nd Lts. were promoted to 1st Lt. (permanent on 1 June 1959).

ACTIVE DUTY ENDS

In early July 1958 I attended my final **Review before "top brass," at Camp Lejeune,** then returned home to Norfolk VA, married my college sweetheart, Miss **Jane Leonard Helm** on 5 July, was released from active duty on 13 July 1958, and began medical school that fall.

From 23 May 1961 until June 1962 I served with a USMC reserve unit, 7th Truck Company, Charlottesville, VA and was promoted to Captain on 1 October 1961. I graduated from the University Of Virginia Medical School in June 1962. I was honorably discharged on 6 July 1965.

As a fellow in Metabolism and Endocrinology at the University of Utah 1966-7, I was involved in a study of Southern Utah residents for thyroid cancer allegedly the result of above ground nuclear testing in Nevada in the 1950s. [101] It was amidst a political firestorm with many millions of dollars spent. The study failed to show any significant increase in thyroid cancer among the "Downwinders." [102] [103]

However, they received compensation anyway. Accurate as well as speculative reporting can also be found in some sources. [104]

During this time Eisenhower's health was not good. He had chronic, high blood pressure. He had suffered a heart attack in September 1955 and a mild stroke that caused a severe headache and mild loss of speech in November 1957. [105] He would retire to his small home in Abilene KS and die in 1969

Until recently I had no idea about why we had our liberty in Athens cancelled or why we went to Crete and combat loaded. I could only guess about the cruiser with a magazine full of nukes, what our mission involved, and why it was suddenly cancelled. For years I kept this information close and remained grateful for its cancelation. Then in 2013 I got curious and looked up "Syria 1957" on-line and found that our mission had been declassified about 2003 because of leaks from British Defense Minister, Edwin Duncan Sandys' (1908-1987) personal papers.

In going over the history of various ships of the 6th fleet and histories of the Marine Units involved, I found no mention of Operation Wappen. Had things happened as planned, our mission would have been a frightful experience. Fortunately cool heads prevailed and it was a "War that Never Was." In talking with others who served the following year in the 1958 Lebanon landings, I found they too had nuclear weapons.

"Ike's Bluff" was "a bold strategy to keep the world at peace by threatening total war." [106] In a March 1955 press conference Eisenhower was asked about the use of nuclear weapons, "I see no reason why they shouldn't be used just exactly as you would use a bullet or anything else." [107] As he later said during his candidacy for a second term: "The problem is not man against man, or nation against nation. It is man against war." [108] During this era, 8" nuclear shells were readily available on both sides.

The Soviet Union likely knew the details and noted our preparedness, and potential intentions. A large fleet is hard to hide. In this situation both sides probably learned caution that saved us from mutually assured destruction during the Cuban Missile Crisis (Oct 1962). Operation Wappen is now on-line for everyone to read; "the cat was out of the bag."

On July 23 1952 a group of "free officers" in the Egyptian Army led by Muhammad Naguib and Gamal Abdel Nasser led a successful coup to overthrow the Egyptian Constitutional Monarchy of King Faruq and eventually expel the British. Two of the major projects that would be undertaken by this group were the takeover of the Suez Canal and the building of the Aswan Dam. The Soviets sensing upheaval in the Middle

East and a possible sphere of influence for them began courting the Arabs, especially the new Egyptian regime.[109]

In 1955 Fedayeen Terrorists veterans of the Arab Israeli War, primarily located in the West Bank of the Jordan River and in bordering parts of Jordan were incorporated into the Egyptian Army.[110] Much of this effort was financed with Soviet money. With the takeover of the Suez Canal in 1956, pan Arab sentiment began to rise in much of the Middle East and this brought with it rise of strict interpretation of the *Korân* among many Arabs. Soviet money began coming into Egypt and Syria. Communist Parties began developing in the Middle East especially Syria. A high degree of Pan Arab sentiment developed and threatened the monarchies of Israel, Saudi Arabia, and Jordan. In the 1950s Iraq was a secular prosperous country with a Constitutional monarchy. It also resisted the pan-Arab / Communist, intolerant religious beliefs that were rising in many of these countries. Iraq fell next on July 14, 1958 when the Hashemite King Faisal II and Ad al-Ilah along with much of the royal family were executed by the Army. [111] Although it was supposedly a republic, the new government more resembled a military dictatorship.

Most of the serious destabilization was happening in the States that bordered Israel – Syria, Egypt, the West Bank and parts of Jordan. With heightening religious tensions that were primarily determinist in ideology, Communism and dictatorships, also determinist were more easily accepted.

According to reports now available, the U.S. and Britain were deeply troubled by these events. Their secret services, the CIA and MI6 began developing plots to overthrow the Syrian government in 1956 and 1957. The first of these was *Operation Straggle.* On July 1, 1956 Wilbur Crain (NSC), Archibald Roosevelt (CIA) met with MB Ilyan, a former Syrian official to plan a potential takeover on October 26, 1956 of the Syrian Government to prevent "communist" influences from spreading. The Syrian Army would lead the coup by taking over Damascus, Aleppo, Homs and Hammah along with frontier posts on the borders of Jordan, Lebanon and Iraq. Colonel Kabbani would lead armored units in the capitol.

In the U.S. a coup was publicly opposed by Secretary of State John Foster Dulles, but privately backed. President Eisenhower allegedly approved of it. However, the whole thing was postponed because of the 6-Day War between Israel and Egypt. At the time we were safely in basic training at Quantico. We knew about the Suez Canal takeover by Egypt on July 26, 1956. There were some rumors that we might begin an accelerated wartime program of training, but this never came to fruition. We continued our peacetime pace until graduation on 12 February 1957 and heard nothing more coming out of the Middle East.

Operation Wappen came shortly after in 1957. Communist activity in Syria was considered to be a threat by both the U.S. and Britain. Wappen, planned by Kermit Roosevelt initially would use about $3 million in bribes to bring down the Syrian Government. However, those receiving the bribes leaked the information to Syrian intelligence sources and the upshot was the deportation of 3 U.S. high officials in Damascus. After the coup had gone awry, fake news reported upwards of 123 MIGs from the Soviet Union shipped into Syria. There were none. In September, about the time we were engaged in Operation Deep Water in Thrace, the U.S. sent a fleet to the Mediterranean (much of it was in fact engaged in Operation Deep Water), sent arms to several Syrian neighbors (presumably Israel, Iraq and Jordan) and suggested that the Turks move 50,000 troops to the Syrian border. An incident was planned to set the whole thing in motion on October 8, however, the Russians stole the show on October 4 by launching sputnik, and on October 9, President Eisenhower had to send the 101st Airborne Division to Little Rock to desegregate the schools. At the same time Secretary of State John Foster Dulles suggested that the Eisenhower Doctrine would apply to the Syrian – Egyptian alliance backed with Soviet money. However, when Iraq and Jordan found that there were no real threats building up in Syria, they pulled out of the deal.

In the meanwhile, there was a plot to assassinate 3 Syrian officials hatched by the United States CIA and the British MI6. Those to be liquidated were: Abdel Hamid al-Sarraj (Syrian chief of Intelligence), Afif al-Bizri (Army Chief of Staff) and Khalid Bakdash (Chief of the Syrian Communist Party). By this time the CIA and MI6 were coordinating the moves. The idea was to finance a "Free Syria Committee", provide weapons to paramilitary groups including the Muslim Brotherhood. Propaganda would report plots emanating from Syria against her neighbors.

These reports would form the rationale for an outside invasion by US Marines – that's us – but we knew nothing of any of this. At that time we were having "conditioning marches" in the White Mountains of Crete, and chasing female non-combatants out of our camps. It would be absolutely essential to convince the people of Syria, Iraq, Jordan, Lebanon and Egypt that there was an emergency in Syria that had to be handled. If there was, we certainly had no information about it. The propaganda plan followed the scenario used earlier in Guatemala (1953) and Iran (1954). All this was finally uncovered in 2003 when secret papers in the possession of Duncan Sandys were exposed.

According to this source, the plan was aborted when Saudi Arabia and Iraq made diplomatic efforts to end the non-crisis. The real reason was probably that none of Syria's neighbors were convinced that anything of significance was happening there. As best I can tell from White House Meetings, Ike decided to bag the whole deal. Besides, Indonesia was becoming a hot spot and needed CIA attention. In addition, the Queen of England was scheduled to arrive in Washington on the 17th of October. So just as suddenly as we arrived we found ourselves headed west at flank speed on the morning of October 17 instead of hitting the beaches. [112]

Carl von Clausewitz said, "*The political object is the goal, war is the means of reaching it, and the means can never be considered in isolation from their purposes.*" He added, "*War is the continuation of politics by other means.*" It is well for all of us to keep this in mind when considering both. [113]

AFTERWORD

Since writing this work a book by Sami Moubayed, *L* 2012 and copywritten in 2013 has come into my possession. It goes into the diplomatic details of October 1957 that may have caused Eisenhower and his cabinet to cancel *Operation Wappen.*

On October 3 Syria issued a statement of friendship with the Turkish Republic. It also declared that the only country likely to attack her was Israel. Martial law had been lifted and there was no call-up for reserves. On October 12 two Soviet warships that had been in Lattakia, Syria sailed home. The US charge d' affaires, Robert Strong "announced that Dulles' policy of isolating Syria, toppling the regime in Damascus or changing its behavior had all ultimately and collectively failed." [114] He hoped for neutrality of the country. In addition, a new ambassador from Syria was about to arrive in the U.S.

Eisenhower had also stated that the situation in Syria had stabilized and that a new ambassador from the U.S., Charles W. Yost had been selected to become the new U.S. Ambassador to Syria. There were hopes that "the conspiracy-filled days of Ambassador James S. Moose – which began under President Adib al Shishakli and lasted under both Presidents Mohammad Tawfeeq ibn Abdul-Lateef al-Atassi and Shukri al-Quwatli, climaxing with the Malki Affair and Operation Straggle – were finally over." [This had been the bribery effort to overthrow the government in 1956.] Our pre-invasion briefing occurred in the late afternoon of October 16. The landing was scheduled for the morning of October 17, but was cancelled sometime between then, probably on direct orders from President Eisenhower.

OFFICIAL ITINERARY – OPERATIONS DEEPWATER & WAPPEN

HEADQUARTERS
3D BATTALION, 6TH MARINES
2D MARINE DIVISION, FMF
CAMP LEJEUNE, N. C.

WJK:lph

30Aug57	Departed Wilmington, North Carolina aboard U.S.S. OLMSTED (APA-188)
16Sep57	Arrived Taranto, Italy
19Sep57	Departed Taranto, Italy
22Sep57	Arrived Gelibolu, Turkey
29Sep57	Departed Seros Bay, Turkey
30Sep57	Arrived Athens, Greece
9Oct57	Departed Athens, Greece
10Oct57	Arrived Souda Bay, Crete
15Oct57	Departed Souda Bay, Crete
18Oct57	Arrived Palermo, Sicily
28Oct57	Departed Palermo, Sicily
1Nov57	Arrived Barcelona, Spain
4Nov57	Departed Barcelona, Spain
6Nov57	Arrived Gibraltar, B.C.C.
6Nov57	Departed Gibraltar, B.C.C.
18Nov57	Arrived and Disembarked Morehead City, North Carolina

W. H. SHIELDS JR
1stLt USMCR
Bn Adjutant

Honorable Discharge

FIDELI CERTA MERCES

from the Armed Forces of the United States of America

This is to certify that

CAPTAIN ROBERT KENT MADDOCK JR. 071383 USMCR

was Honorably Discharged from the

United States Marine Corps

on the 6TH *day of* JULY 1965 *This certificate is awarded as a testimonial of Honest and Faithful Service*

Robert H. B. Baldwin

ROBERT H. B. BALDWIN
Under Secretary of the Navy

ENDNOTES

Color and black and white pictures used in this work were taken at the time by the author. Some are from the Marine Corps School's History of the Fourth Basic Class, an un-copy written publication for which the author was a photographer. Art work is by Raija Pönkänen.

Author & Illustrator
Robert & Raija Maddock 2008

ABBREVIATIONS & MILITARY ORGANIZATION

FBI – Federal Bureau of Investigation

CIA – Central Intelligence Agency

NROTC – Naval Reserve Officers Training Corps

BOQ – bachelor officers' quarters

NATO – North Atlantic Treaty Organization

D-Day – June 6, 1944

MI6–British Secret Service (Military Intelligence Section 6)

CIA – Central Intelligence Agency

AD – Anno Domini (year of our Lord)

CE – Christian Era

Bc – Before Christ

BCE – Before the Christian Era

Blitz – German for "lightning"

CIC – Counter Intelligence Agency

OSS – Office of Strategic Services

NKVD – "*Narodny Komissarat Vnutrennikh Del" People's Commissariat of Internal Affairs – Russian secret service.*

CIC – Counter Intelligence Corps

Ike – Nickname for General & President Eisenhower

IED – Improvised Explosive Device

USSR – Union of Soviet Socialist Republics (Russia)

U.S. MEDALS FOR COMBAT BRAVERY IN RANKING ORDER

CMH – Congressional Medal of Honor

DSC – Distinguished Service Cross & Navy Cross

Silver Star

Bronze Star

MARINE CORPS MILITARY ORGANIZATION DURING THE COLD WAR

Army –3 or more Divisions – Commanded by a 3 or 4 star Lieutenant General or full General

Division – 1st Mar Div, 2nd Mar Div, 3rd Mar Div – A Division consists of 3 regiments often led by a 2 star Major General

Brigade – a task force of more than one Regiment; led by a 1 star Brigadier General.

Regiment – consists of 3 Battalions numbered numerically & led by a Colonel.

Battalion – consists of 3 companies designated numerically & led by a Lt Col or Major.

Company – consists of 3 Platoons (@ 200 men) led by a Captain; designated alphabetically for all companies within the Regiment Thus 1st Bn has companies A, B, C and 2nd Bn has D, E, F, etc.

Platoon – consists of 3 squads of about 13 men each; led by a lieutenant

Each of the above units includes a headquarters group and often a heavy weapons detachment.

Battalions within a regiment might be designated "3-6" meaning 3rd Battalion, 6th Marine Regiment

F-2-6 would mean Fox Company, 2nd Battalion, 6th Marine Regiment. 3-6 would mean 3rd Battalion 6th Marine Regiment.

Artillery is a supporting arm and arranged in batteries of six 105mm or 155mm howitzers. A battery is about the size of a company with @150 men and supports a Battalion of infantry. 10th Marines was an artillery Regiment in support of 2nd Mar Div. F-2-10 would be Fox Battery 2nd Bn, 10th Marine Regiment and supported 3-6.

This tri-partite form of military organization dates back to the late 16th Century and the development of the Spanish Tercio.

ROMAN 1ST AND 2ND CENTURIES AD ARMY ORGANIZATION [115]

Smallest to largest organization:

1. Contubernium consisted of 8 men
2. Century – had 10 contubernii led by a Centurion
3. Cohort had 6 Centuries @ 480 men; led by a senior centurion
4. Legion – 10 Cohorts with the first cohort containing 5 double Centuries. It was led by a Legatus – often politically appointed
5. Tribunes were political appointees leading armies or task groups.

The Roman Army also had Cavalry and Auxiliary troops managing supply, engineering (siege works, roads and bridges) plus "heavy weapons."

REFERENCES

1. http://en.wikipedia.org/wiki/Operation_Deep_Water
2. http://en.wikipedia.org/wiki/CIA_activities_in_Syria
3. http://en.wikipedia.org/wiki/Operation_Deep_Water
4. http://en.wikipedia.org/wiki/CIA_activities_in_Syria
5. Wilcox RK. *Target Patton.* Regnery Pub. Washington DC. 2008.
6. http://www.fordham.edu/halsall/mod/churchill-iron.asp
7. Wilcox RK. *Target Patton: the Plot To Assassinate General George S Patton.* Regnery Pub Inc. Washington. 2008 Pg. 210.
8. Wilcox, RK. Op. Cit. Pgs.118-120.
9. O'Reilly & Dugard *Killing Patton.* Henry Holt & Co. New York 2014 pg. 241-2; 261
10. Wilcox, RK. Op.Cit. Pg. 121.
11. Wilcox, RK. *Op.Cit.* Pgs.222-3.
12. .http://www.skubik.com/Death%20of%20Patton%20_%20S%20J%20Skubik.pdf
13. Wilcox RK. Op. Cit. Pg. 121.
14. Wilcox, RK. Op. Cit. Pgs.303-312.
15. Wilcox, RK. *Op. Cit.* Pg. 371.
16. http://en.wikipedia.org/wiki/Henry_Thomas_Harrison
17. http://en.wikipedia.org/wiki/Cambridge_Five
18. Skubik,SJ. *The Murder of General Patton.* Skubik Pub, Bennington NH. 1993. Pg. 4.
19. http://en.wikipedia.org/wiki/List_of_Soviet_agents_in_the_United_States#The_.22Berg.22_.E2.80.93_.22Art.22_Group
20. http://www.imdb.com/character/ch0028822/quotes
21. People's Commissariat of Internal Affairs – Narodnyy Komissariat Vnutrennikh Del.
22. Maddock RK, The 1300 Years' War: The evolution of Judeo-Christianity and Islam and their associated warfare. Vol 1. Xlibris. 2016. USA. Pgs. 441-464.

23. **Ibid Pg.32**
24. **Maddock RK. *The 1300 Years' War: the Evolution of Judeo-Christianity and Islam and Their Associated Warfare.* 2 Volumes. Xlibris. 2017. USA**
25. **Maddock RK. Op. Cit. Vol 1. Pg. 94, 99-102**
26. **Ibid Pgs. 338-40.**
27. **http://en.wikipedia.org/wiki/Pareto_principle**
28. **http://en.wikipedia.org/wiki/Columbian_Exchange**
29. **http://en.wikipedia.org/wiki/Black_Death**
30. **Maddock RK. *The 1300 Years' War.* Vol 2, Xlibris 2017 USA Pg. 203.**
31. **http://en.wikipedia.org/wiki/Alexis_de_Tocqueville#On_US_slavery.2C_Blacks_and_Indians**
32. **http://en.wikipedia.org/wiki/History_of_California#Annexation_of_California_.281846-1847.29**
33. **Marx K & Engels F. Manifesto of the Communist Party, International Publishers. New York 1948 Pg. 9.**
34. **Ibid Pgs. 26-29.**
35. **http://www.brainyquote.com/quotes/quotes/r/rahmemanue409199.html**
36. **Marx K & Engels F. Op. Cit. Pg44.**
37. **Hopkirk P. *Foreign Devils on the Silk Road.* John Murray. London 1982.**
38. **Hopkirk P. *Trespassers on the Roof of the World: the Secret Exploration of Tibet.* JP Tarcher Inc. Los Angeles. 1982.**
39. **Tzu, Sun. *The Art of War*, Translated by Samuel B Griffith. Oxford University Press, New York, 1963 Pg. 73**
40. **Tzu, Sun *The Art of War*: Complete Texts and Commentaries. Translated by Cleary. Shambhala Pub Inc. Boston, 2000. Pg. 22.**
41. **Twining M. *No Bended Knee.* Presidio, 1996. Pgs. 147-158**
42. ***O'Donnell JP. The Corps' Struggle for Survival. Marine Corps Gazette. Aug 2000 Pgs. 90-96***
43. **http://en.wikipedia.org/wiki/Battle_of_Chosin_Reservoir**
44. https://archive.org/details/WiththeMarinesatTarawa
45. **http://en.wikipedia.org/wiki/Nellie_Bly**
46. **http://en.wikipedia.org/wiki/Ottoman_public_debt**
47. **http://www.jewishvirtuallibrary.org/jsource/History/Suez_War.html**

48. Talbot D. *The Devils Chessboard: Allen Dulles the CIA and the Rise of America's Secret Government.* Harper Collins. New York 2015.Pgs 250-251.
49. https://www.theguardian.com/news/2000/jun/13/guardianobituaries.haroldjackson
50. http://en.wikipedia.org/wiki/Kermit_Roosevelt#Military_service_in_World_War_I
51. Talbot D. *The Devil's Chessboard.* Harper Collins. New York 2015. Pgs 250.
52. http://en.wikipedia.org/wiki/The_Ballad_of_East_and_West
53. Maddock, RK Op.Cit. Vol 2 Pg297.
54. Maddock, RK Op.Cit. Vol 1 Pgs. 98-99 Vol 2. Pgs. 292-297.
55. http://www.womeninthescriptures.com/2010/11/real-meaning-of-term-help-meet.html
56. Maddock, RK Op.Cit. Vol 1 Pgs. 94-96; Vol 2 Pgs.301-2
57. Maddock, RK Op. Cit. Vol 1 pg. 80.
58. http://en.wikipedia.org/wiki/Fratricide
59. Maddock, RK. Op, Cit. Vol 2. Pgs. 244-251.
60. Maddock, RK, Op. Cit. Vol 1. Pg. 11.
61. Maddock, RK, Op. Cit. Vol 1. Pgs. 121-122
62. http://muslimmatters.org/2012/01/10/part-ii-the-decline-of-the-ottoman-empire/
63. http://en.wikipedia.org/wiki/Auspicious_Incident
64. http://en.wikipedia.org/wiki/Ottoman_Public_Debt_Administration
65. Maddock, RK. Op. Cit. Vol 2. Pgs. 281-3.
66. Ben Fenton, "Macmillan backed Syria assassination plot: Documents show White House and No 10 Conspired over oil-fueled invasion plan." *The Guardian*, 26 September 2003.
67. http://en.wikipedia.org/wiki/CIA_activities-in-Syria#Operation_Wappen.2C_1957
68. http://ontos.homestead.com/back.html
69. Mc Donald JM. Colonel Joseph R. "Bull" Fisher: A Marine's Marine. *Leatherneck* 89:12. Dec 2006.
70. http://kbaymarine.com/images/Colonel_Joseph_R_Bull_Fisher.pdf
71. http://www.homeofheroes.com/brotherhood/chosin.html
72. http://en.wikipedia.org/wiki/Canister_shot
73. http://en.wikipedia.org/wiki/Battle_of_Chosin_Reservoir

74. http://www.24hourcampfire.com/ubbthreads/ubbthreads.php/topics/2981034/6
Re: any Chosin Marines on the fire? [Re: crossfireoops]
75. http://en.wikipedia.org/wiki/Battle_of_Chosin_Reservoir
76. Personal communications, Dick Asher commander of Ontos detachment, 6th Marines, Operation Deep Water.
77. http://ontos.homestead.com/back.html
78. http://en.wikipedia.org/wiki/Iron_Triangle_(Korea)
79. Picture taken by author in 1950 – Snowy-Sides Peak ID
80. Picture taken by John E Hayes' crew 1903-4 intersection Shoshone Ave & Main St. Twin Falls, ID.
81. http://www.wendoverairbase.com/
82. Saunders BF. *The United States and Arab Nationalism: the Syrian case 1953-1960.* Praeger Pub. Westport CT.1996 Pg. 64.
83. http://en.wikipedia.org/wiki/Austin_Shofner
84. USS Olmsted APA 188 National Archive photo no. 80-G-688815
85. USS Chilton APA 38 National Archive photo no. 80-G-214340
86. USS Fort Snelling LSD 30 National Archives photo no. 80-G-693721
87. Buckner DN. *A Brief History of the 10th Marines.* Dept of the Navy. Washington DC. 1981. Pg. 95.
88. USS Terrebonne Parish LST 1156 National Archives photo no. 80-G-668006
89. http://www.marines.mil/Portals/59/Publications/A%20Brief%20History%20of%20the%2010th%20Marines%20PCN%2019000308400_3.pdf
90. http://en.wikipedia.org.advanc.io/wiki/CIA_activities_in_Syria
Blum, *Killing Hope* (1995), Common Courage Press. Monroe. Pg. 90–91.
91. http://en.wikipedia.org/wiki/3rd_Battalion_6th_Marines
92. http://www.pbs.org/wgbh/nova/parthenon/rest-nf.html
93. See Appointment Records – Eisenhower Library Records http://eisenhower.archives.gov/research/online_documents/presidential_appointment-books/1957/October_1957.pdf
94. http://www.navsource.org/archives/04/123/04123.htm
95. https://en.wikipedia.org/wiki/John_S._McCain_Jr.
96. https://en.wikipedia.org/wiki/USS_John_S._McCain_(DDG-56)

97. http://www.legacy.com/obituaries/atlanta/obituary.aspx?n=james-william-benson&pid=1941912#sthash.yzy5KyYz.dpuf
98. USS Albany CA 123 National Archives photo no. 80-G-429233
99. https://en.wikipedia.org/wiki/Nuclear_artillery
100. https://en.wikipedia.org/wiki/Nuclear_weapon_yield
101. http://www.ncbi.nlm.nih.gov/pmc/articles/PMC1530660/
102. Blum W. *Killing Hope*, Common Courage Press. Monroe Maine.1995. Pg.3.
103. Rallison ML et al. Cohort study of thyroid disease near the Nevada Test Site: a preliminary report. Health Phys. 1990 Nov 59(5): 739-46.
104. Blum W. *Killing Hope*, Common Courage Press. Monroe Maine.1995. Pgs. 91-2.
105. Talbot D. *The Devil's Chessboard.* Harper Collins. New York. 2015. Pg. 245
106. Talbot D. *The Devil's Chessboard.* Pg. 242
107. Ibid Pg. 243
108. Ibid Pg.243
109. https://en.wikipedia.org/wiki/Egyptian_revolution_of_1952
110. https://en.wikipedia.org/wiki/Fedayeen#Egypt
111. https://en.wikipedia.org/wiki/20th-century_history_of_Iraq#Republic_of_Iraq
112. https://en.wikipedia.org/wiki/CIA_activities_in_Syria#Attempted_regime_change.2C_1956.E2.80.9357
113. http://www.brainyquote.com/quotes/quotes/c/carlvoncla138192.html
114. Moubayed, S. *Syria and the USA: Washington's Relations with Damascus from Wilson to Eisenhower* IB Tauris New York 2012 Pg. 170
115. Webster, G. *The Roman Imperial Army*, Barnes and Noble, New York 1994 Pg. 115

INDEX

C

D

E

F

G

H

S

T

CPSIA information can be obtained
at www.ICGtesting.com
Printed in the USA
FFHW010848220519
52597069-58069FF

9 781643 675312